D0112023

The Art of
Stopping

Also by David Kundtz

Nothing's Wrong: A Man's Guide to
Managing His Feelings

Quiet Mind: One Minute Mindfulness

Awakened Mind: One Minute Wake Up Calls

Being Present: A Book of Daily Reflections

Coming To: A Biomythograph

The Art of
Stopping

How to Be Still When
You Have to Keep Going

David Kundtz

Foreword by Richard Carlson

Conari
Press

CORAL GABLES

Cover and Interior Layout Design: Jermaine Lau

Published by Conari Press, an imprint of Mango Media Inc.

For permission requests, please contact the publisher at:

Mango Publishing Group
2850 Douglas Road, 2nd Floor
Coral Gables, FL 33134 USA
info@mango.bz

For special orders, quantity sales, course adoptions and corporate sales, please email the publisher at sales@mango.bz. For trade and wholesale sales, please contact Ingram Publisher Services at customer.service@ingramcontent.com or +1.800.509.4887.

The Art of Stopping: How to Be Still When You Have to Keep Going

ISBN: (p) 978-1-64250-439-2 (e) 978-1-64250-440-8

BISAC: SEL016000, SELF-HELP / Personal Growth / Happiness

LCCN: Pending

All acknowledgments of permission to reprint previously published material can be found on pp. 247-248, which constitute an extension of this copyright page.

Chart on page 145 John Lomibao Design

To the memory of my father whose example
taught me about Stopping.
To the memory of my mother who encouraged me to write.

Table of Contents

Foreword

When I first looked at *The Art of Stopping: How to Be Still When You Have to Keep Going*, I realized immediately that I was in familiar territory. In fact, it didn't take me long to locate in my own work a very specific expression of what *Stopping* is all about: "Virtually every day, I stop whatever I'm doing to enjoy the sunrise…" (from *Don't Sweat the Small Stuff…and It's All Small Stuff*). And this is just one of many examples. Yes, Stopping as defined by Dr. Kundtz—doing nothing in order to wake up and remember who you are—is something that has been part of my life for a long time.

What we owe David Kundtz is credit for conceptualizing a simple yet profound reality and offering to us an elegant and powerful tool for finding the serenity and stillness that so easily escapes us as we cope with too-busy lives.

Stopping is a happy marriage of the riches of many of the world's contemplative and mystical traditions with the insight and awareness of contemporary psychology. Just what the world needs right now, it seems to me.

Finally, because it gives us perspective, because it encourages us to put first things first, and because it keeps us awake and aware, *Stopping* is an ideal way to remember something important about the vast majority of things that bother and upset us: it's all small stuff.

Richard Carlson, PhD

Author's Introduction

How to be still when you have to keep going—that's what this book is about. It offers practical help in coping with the complicated and challenging world of the twenty-first century, which, as this book goes to press, is experiencing the global crisis of Covid-19. The pandemic came into an already struggling world that seemed to be losing its sense of fairness and decency, and was foundering about in search of leadership and unity.

This is, however, the world we actually live in; and we have no choice: we have to keep going, often now through unknown territory with no precedents to follow.

Thus, the art of Stopping: a process of accessing your own untapped inner wisdom and strength.

Stopping is doing nothing, as much as possible, with the purpose of becoming more awake, remembering who you are, and what you want. Its elements are Stillpoints, Stopovers, and Grinding Halts.

It is based on the belief that only if you have enough stillness and relaxation in your life are you able to access your ever-present inner wisdom and live the life you want, the life you choose to live. Otherwise that wisdom never finds its voice, is drowned out by distractions, and you forget what is truly important to you, only to live a default version of life that the unenlightened and wild forces of the world dictate. In other words, your life becomes a tragedy.

The title of this book is *The Art of Stopping*. Stopping is an art rather than a process or an activity. It is an art because it depends on your own creativity and style and it is based on accessing your own rich and wonderful inner life. Your experience of Stopping is your unique creation.

Stopping is compatible with all faiths or none, has no doctrines or politics, and is elegantly simple.

Welcome to your true life. Welcome to Stopping.

David Kundtz
Kensington, California

PART I
Stopping at the Speed of Light

CHAPTER 1
Facing the Mountain of Too Much

"The dogmas of the quiet past, are inadequate to the stormy present...As our case is new, so we must think anew and act anew."

—Abraham Lincoln

"It's too much," Mary Helen told me, "way too much. I just can't deal with it all!" Then she gave in to tears. Mary Helen, a successful and intelligent woman of thirty-eight, with a thriving career and a loving family, was close to the end of her rope.

Any observer in my counseling office that day would have seen that Mary Helen was in trouble: anxious, stressed, unfocused, irritable, unable to sleep, over-whelmed by life, and frustrated with her inability to manage it. She was angry at herself for her inability to cope and angry at me because I was the one to whom she had admitted it.

Although she was not aware of it, she did know what the problem was. It was the first thing she said: "It's too much." Upon further exploration, I found no underlying psychosis, no debilitating personality disorder, no family-of-origin dysfunction making a sudden midlife appearance, and no marriage about to crash on the rocks of incompatibility. Just that life had become too much.

Just that life had become too much? Hardly. Although the problem may seem well known, its vastness, depth, and long-term implications are still far from our conscious recognition. As with any hidden enemy, the contemporary problem of too much has its way with all of us. The damage is extremely severe and is sometimes even life threatening.

"Being overwhelmed means that your life or work is overpowering you."
—Daphne Michaels, writer

Do you sometimes feel like Mary Helen, overwhelmed or emotionally numbed by the pace and sheer quantity of life? Are you reluctantly prevented by your overloaded schedule from keeping your true priorities? Do you feel unable to do all the things you need to do and still have enough time for yourself? Have you come to realize that it's been too long since you've enjoyed real, satisfying, and regular leisure? If so, you've found the right book.

Do you have a desire to give more attention to the spiritual aspects of your life—your truly important meanings and values—but have been frustrated in trying to transform that desire into a real practice? You will find nourishment here.

Or have you been frustrated with complicated, time-consuming, or impractical systems of meditation and slowing down that don't really work for you? You can anticipate success through the suggestions found in the practice of Stopping.

Most of us in this hurry up, instant message/text/tweet/email world of immediate response are feeling the same sense of overload that my client Mary Helen felt. Indeed, the primary challenge to successful human life in the post-modern, post-millennial world is the challenge of too much: too much to do; too much to cope with; too much distraction; too much noise; too much demanding our attention; even, for many of us, too many opportunities and too many choices. Too much of everything for the time and energy available.

As we all have been noticing, at least on a subliminal level, the choices, demands, and complexities of life increase with every passing year. We have more to be, more to do, more places to go, and more things we want or need to accomplish. But the day remains twenty-four hours; the year, the same twelve months. The amount of activity constantly increases, but both the amount of time into which it must fit and the human energy with which it must be met, at best, remain the same.

Even though my client Mary Helen named her problem—"It's way too much. I just can't deal with it all"—she didn't recognize it, first, as something serious and, second, as something new. Rather, she saw it just as one more of life's irritations that she should be able to deal with. This attitude reveals a key characteristic of the problem of too much: It passes itself off as something it is not. It says, "I am the same old problem you have been dealing with all your life, you can handle me." But the reality is that we can't—and believing we can, is part of the problem.

Why don't we see it coming? The answer is as simple as it is clear: it is masquerading, and the purpose of a masquerade is to make you think it's something else. We are all like Mary Helen, saying to ourselves, "This should not be a serious problem!" Because it looks and feels like the same old problem of being just too busy and, in the past, we have been able to handle it with the coping strategies available to us, we miss its seriousness and power.

It's time to rip off the mask from the problem of too much and reveal the seriously damaging monster that is destroying too many lives and too many families. Modern life has become impossible to cope with in the same old ways we learned as children and young adults.

That's because the sheer amount of too much also makes it a new and essentially different challenge. Consider this for a moment, because at first it might not seem evident: Precisely because of the very large volume of the same old thing, it has become essentially different. It is not just a larger amount of the same thing but is something entirely new.

It's like the evolution of a pile of rocks into a mountain. At some point in its history it stops being a pile of rocks and starts being a mountain. When exactly does that happen? The transition point would be difficult to determine. Does this last addition finally make it a mountain, or must we wait for more? So it is with the problem of too much: it has become what it is over a long period of time. For most of us, the point at which too much has become a mountain is long past. What used to be a pile of rocks has become the Mountain of Too Much.

It is vital to recognize this mountain as new because it is the newness that signifies the need for different coping strategies to conquer it. The tools needed to conquer a pile of rocks are very different from those demanded by a mountain. So it is as we face the Mountain of Too Much. A sturdy pair of shoes is sufficient for a pile of rocks, but an imposing peak demands carabiners, belaying systems, and training in specific skills.

Mary Helen, my bright, normally fun-loving and competent client, was truly puzzled. "Why can't I deal with this? I have always been able to cope, even when things have been difficult. Why not now?" But this was a new and challenging mountain, not just the same old pile of rocks she had walked over many times before. But *that* was what she needed to see.

So it is with all of us—we keep dealing with the problem of too much in the same old ways. As a result, we are overstressed, overloaded, overtired, and unable to solve the serious problems and challenges that are a direct result of our revved-up pace of life. It's time to learn a different way to face our Mountain of Too Much and to trade in our old ways of coping for new ones.

CHAPTER 2
Why Cramming and Cutting Don't Work

"No matter how fast we go, no matter how many comforts we forgo...there never seems to be enough time."

—Jay Walljasper

In the past, we used two ways of coping with the challenge of too much: we crammed things in or we cut things out. These are natural, normal, and effective responses to life at a certain pace.

Cramming is trying to fit more and more into the same, limited time and space using the same, limited energy and stamina. Until the pile of rocks changed into the Mountain of Too Much, cramming worked just fine: We became more efficient and more productive. We learned to manage our time better, to move faster, and to sprint through our day without pausing for breath. But that was before we reached the critical mass of too much. Now it causes us to be overwhelmed and stuffed to overfull; thus, we are left frustrated and feeling like we have no room left for ourselves. Whenever I feel this stuffed feeling, I often show it through moodiness, irritability, and spiritual malaise.

Think of packing your suitcase. Have you ever tried to cram things in? You cram and cram and even resort to sitting on it to force it closed, but there is a moment when, with just one more pair of socks, the suitcase will not close. And even if we manage to jam the suitcase shut, we may rip its seams or risk it popping open in mid journey. Think of yourself as that suitcase: Your seams are ripping and your emotional insides are bursting out and spilling into the middle of your day. That's the point we're at. Cramming no longer works. There is simply too much to fit in.

"Never before have we had so little time in which to do so much."
—Franklin D. Roosevelt

Cutting out is excluding things from our lives to make more room for new demands. We become good at prioritizing: we drop old friends to make room for taking our kids to soccer, we eliminate lunch to get a little more work done, we cut short our days off to catch up on a report, and we wake up an hour early to have time for exercise. But this works only to a certain point. Finally, you can cut out no more. You get down to the essentials: work, personal responsibilities, and a necessary amount of sleep and social time. When demands from work or family crises intervene, leisure time, exercise, social life, and days off go out the window. Finally, there comes a time when there is nothing to cut and still too much to do. Our health— mental and physical—suffers. We voice the complaint that I hear most often in my seminars on stress: We feel as though we are moving through life, but not actually *experiencing* it. As you probably know from your own life, cutting things out just no longer works.

The Mountain of Too Much is new and therefore calls for new skills. It's long past the time to let go of these once-effective responses. They are ineffective habits of behavior. They also constitute a form of denial, a refusal to face up to a situation too painful or disturbing to acknowledge, in this case the problem of too much. Besides being futile, these habits are robbing us of the pleasure of life. But there is something new that you can learn to do.

I call it Stopping.

CHAPTER 3
Doing Nothing

"I have a very full and busy life and occasionally I am asked, 'Scotty, how can you do all that you do?' The most telling reply I can give is, 'Because I spend at least two hours a day doing nothing.' "

—M. Scott Peck, physician and writer

The first time I became aware of Stopping, I was hiding. I was on the run and felt lost. I was trying to figure out what to do with my life and didn't really know what was happening to me or how it would all turn out.

I had been a successful and content clergyman for fifteen years, but all of a sudden I was in crisis. Nothing felt right anymore. My enthusiasm for my vocation had abandoned me. For the first time in my life I felt lonely. I avoided responsibilities, denied what was happening, and made some foolish decisions. Finally, not knowing what to do, I stopped doing everything. For a month, I escaped to a small, isolated cabin, perched high on a hill overlooking the Pacific Ocean on the Northern California coast, to figure it out.

I just stopped. And in so doing, I found my way again. I didn't stop on purpose, but it was the best thing I could have done for myself. It was not until much later, after many occasions of Stopping, some as short as ten seconds and others as long as a month, that I became conscious of its value and could actually define it:

Stopping is doing nothing, as much as possible, for a definite period of time, for the purpose of becoming more fully awake and remembering who you are and what you want.

This is the simple practice upon which this book is built, a new skill to replace cramming and cutting that can help deal with the Mountain of Too Much. Doing nothing should not be confused with a total lack of activity. Doing nothing is indeed doing something important. It's allowing life to happen—your life. Doing nothing is something quite profound.

The ultimate purpose of Stopping is to ensure that when we do go, we go in the direction that we want and that we are not just reacting to the pace of our lives, but choosing, moment by moment, what's best. The ultimate reason for Stopping is going. Going is what we of the industrialized Western world are known for. It's what we do best: get on with business, get things done, accomplish feats, and assume roles of leadership and power. Thus, Stopping at first glance might not seem so desirable, it may even appear to be opposed to our fundamental values. But, not only is it *not* against these values, Stopping maintains and cultivates them. Without being awake and remembering our values and identity—in other words, without Stopping—our going can get us into deep trouble.

I cannot emphasize this enough: Stopping is not a value *in itself*, because the ultimate purpose of Stopping is always to make the going right, to make sure our life goes in the direction that we want it to.

Stopping, even in its shortest form, allows you to realize the essential meanings of your life and to consistently remember what is truly important to you so you can keep your priorities in order and up to date. It helps you know what you want to achieve and how you want to behave.

"Many of us have been running all our lives.
Practice stopping."
—Thich Nhat Hahn, monk, Zen master

Stopping works where cramming and cutting don't because it calls a time-out and gives you the freedom to reorganize your life according to your own rules, to recognize your true priorities. It creates an oasis where the turbulent waters caused by the demands of daily life can quiet and where, in the stillness, you can again see your own reflection. It gives you time to *be*, not just to *do*.

Stopping is born of personal experience and, like many useful ideas, came to me because I needed it so badly. In most cases, we don't stop until we feel overwhelmed and don't know where to turn. For some reason, when I got to the end of my rope, I just did nothing and waited, not out of any virtuous inclination, not because I thought the waiting would solve anything, but because I didn't know what else to do.

Now I can look back and see the value in that time of waiting: There were moments, short and long, in which I remembered some important information about myself, became more awake to my life, and became aware of all the aspects involved in the issues I was dealing with. Stopping helped me get going again, but going in a focused and determined way, rather than a scattered and chaotic one.

So this book is about Stopping, and specifically about Stopping when you feel you have to keep going. This kind of quieting and self-remembering is designed specifically to fit the needs of people who must live their lives in a world ruled by cell phones and social media as well as global warming/climate change, wild and often brutal politics, and record high levels of social meanness, anxiety, and depression. My hope is that Stopping will contribute to your achieving your desired levels of wisdom and caring in a turbulent, troublesome world.

CHAPTER 4

A Fast Train on the Fast Track

"The fast-paced rhythm of modern life conditions us to skim the surface of experience, then quickly move on to something new."

—Stephan Rechtschaffen, physician

Stopping is not slowing down. There are many books on slowing down the frantic pace of life. This is not one of them, even though an important aspect of Stopping—even one of the reasons for Stopping—is, in fact, to slow down. The process of Stopping is different from the process of slowing down. Trying to slow down rarely slows you down. We have been trying to do that for many years now; it generally doesn't work. It's like trying to cut down on smoking: in a short time you end up where you started, except more frustrated.

Slowing down often doesn't work because everything around us is going so fast. We get revved up even if we don't want to be. In his book *Time Shifting,* Stephan Rechtschaffen, MD, writes about *entrainment,* which he describes as an unconscious "process that governs how various rhythms fall into sync with one another." For example, if you were to place two out-of-sync pendulum clocks next to one another, in a short time they would be exactly in sync. "The same principle works," says Rechtschaffen, "with atomic particles, the tides, and human beings." With human beings? That's a remarkable idea. We pick up each other's rhythms and the accumulated rhythms of the world around us. If most of the rhythms around us are fast, so are ours, automatically. That's entrainment. The word can also mean "getting on a train."

We have all boarded the train, the fast train on the fast track, and the process of entrainment is not under our conscious control. That's why trying to slow down doesn't slow us down. It's not because we're weak willed or quitters; it's because we're on a fast train where we're the passengers and not the engineer.

We are all riding on a fast train that is traveling down a predetermined track, gathering speed as it goes, and we have been on it for a long time. We can't get to the engineer because the engineer is protected by loyal guards. Or perhaps there really is no engineer; the train is run by a computer. Many of us want to slow down. Some want to get off the train. Others are so used to the speed that they don't notice it. A few love the speed and want to increase it. The few who love the speed are the only ones who get their way. Most of us stare blankly out the window, barely seeing the world flying by and feeling helpless.

Fortunately, there is something we can do about it. Stopping can get us off the train, can separate us from the speeded-up rhythms of those around us, and can bring us into rhythms of our own choosing, which, it's important to note, may well include *some* time on the fast train. Stopping can roll us into the roundhouse for refreshment and cooling off so we can make sure that, when we get aboard again, we're on the right track, going in the right direction, and have a very intimate working relationship with the engineer.

"We entrain to the rhythms around us all the time, although we are not aware of it most of the time."
—Frank Lipman, MD

Entrainment helps to explain the amazingly short attention span of most of us these days. We get our information in sound bites: many brief, skeletal bones of facts. We don't have time to read in depth or to linger over the newspaper. It seems also to have something to say about our fad-driven, screen-based society. As soon as one idea, trend, fashion, or person becomes popular, it is quickly dropped for whatever next demands our attention. Whether it is valuable or vulgar seems to make no difference; it's just the next view out the window of the fast train. Fad-driven and screen-obsessed culture engenders tense and frenetic citizens who find themselves, unwittingly, screaming through the night on the fast train and trying to figure out, "How did I get here?"

Stopping can bring us both an answer and a solution.

CHAPTER 5
Stopping at the Speed of Light

"It's good to have an end to journey toward; but it's the
journey that matters, in the end."

—Ursula K. Le Guin, writer

Stopping is paradoxical. It would seem that if one just stops—
that is, does nothing—it would be a waste of time. Indeed, a
way to describe doing nothing is "wasting time." And when
you feel stressed and have too much to do, doing nothing may
feel like the worst approach. But paradoxically, doing nothing
turns out to be not only not a waste of time but some of the
most significant time you can spend, even if it is only for
one minute.

This idea flies in the face of current belief and practice; "Do
more and do it more quickly" is what we hear. But it is exactly
this attitude that has made us overwhelmed. What we've been
doing isn't working.

The kind of Stopping that I am suggesting is done while
moving *at the speed of light*. Stopping while moving at the speed
of light is a paradox: To stop on the one hand and to go at the
speed of light on the other are contradictory statements that
create so radical a paradox that they appear to be an oxymoron.

In other words, it doesn't make sense—unless you see it paradoxically. Then it is transformed into an exquisite, inviting, alluring, and richly textured truth: Time spent doing nothing allows us to awaken what is most meaningful and valuable to us.

This soulful paradox is actually based on a scientific paradox. The amazing fact is that objects moving at the speed of light no longer experience time. In other words, at the speed of light, time stands still. Scientists assure me that these are true and accurate statements. I don't pretend to understand them scientifically, but I like them. And I like to apply them to Stopping: Stopping is time standing still or standing still in time.

Stopping at the speed of light acknowledges that the Stopping takes place within the context of a very fast world that waits for no one and which, if you can't keep up, will leave you behind. It also acknowledges something that many people who teach spirituality are often resistant to accept: going fast is not necessarily bad. Many of the "technologies that promote speed are essentially good. The historical record is that human beings have never, ever opted for slowness," says Jay Walljasper, writer and editor. "When I hear friends complain that their lives move too fast, they're not talking about a wholesale rejection of speed so much as a wish that they could spend more of their time involved in slow, contemplative activities." The problem, of course, is that there is way too much of one and not enough of the other. Stopping can restore the balance.

Many of us love the revved-up beat of dance music, the fast-breaking action of basketball, or the quick-paced energy of a video game, but we don't want to live all our lives at that pace.

"A balanced life," says Walljasper, "with intervals of creative frenzy giving way to relaxed tranquility—is what people crave." Yes—and that's what Stopping is about.

The ultimate purpose of Stopping is going. But Stopping at the speed of light is not an unfulfilling, endless switching back and forth between going too fast and being dead still. Rather it brings its results, its gifts, to the person, not to the rate of speed. Its wonders are worked in the soul and thus are part of the person no matter what the speed of the moment.

Stopping ten times in a very hectic, emotionally demanding day doesn't feel like a jerky ride. Rather, it feels like a smooth flow moving in a balanced way through the day. The results are that you come to the end of the day not limp, exhausted, and depressed but okay and ready to continue with enthusiasm.

CHAPTER 6
Intentional Living: From Routine to Choice

"If families just let the culture happen to them, they end up fat, addicted, broke, with a house full of junk and no time."

—Mary Pipher, psychologist

It used to be that people didn't need Stopping *per se* because the natural rhythms of life provided sufficient time for them to achieve a sense of balance between quiet work and active work. There were busy times and leisure times and they tended to balance one another. It was just the way life was.

This balance was probably the common experience of our grandparents or great-grandparents. The pace of life allowed for time in between events: the time walking to school, to a neighbor's, or to church, and the time of solitary work around the house, shop, or farm. Life on the land was hard, but there were long stretches of winter when people were homebound, and the pace slowed.

I can remember as a boy loving to drive out with my grandfather to his pig farm in rural northern Ohio. This was in the late '40s. To me, my grandfather was bigger than life. He was serious but kindly, had an Irish twinkle in his eye, and always greeted me with, "*Davit me bye!*" My mother was reluctant to let me go with him because I would invariably come home a mess and late for dinner. My grandfather would spend hours checking on the pigs and talking to the farm manager who ran the place. But what I did was truly magical. I wandered around the farm—probably never out of eyeshot, or at least earshot, of my grandfather—and explored everything: the barn, the old, rusted machinery, the pigs (I never got too close), and the fields. I was doing nothing but fussin' around, poking about, loafing, hangin' out, and kickin' back.

For most of us (isn't it sad to think of kids deprived of these aimless times?) such moments don't happen very often anymore. They aren't built into the pace of life; we're just too busy. Picture these scenes in your mind's eye:

On a leafy street in a small town, suburb, or residential part of the city, a woman in her fifties, with graying hair, a calm look on her face, and wearing a simple house dress and apron, is seated in a rocking chair on her front porch on a warm summer afternoon. Her kids are somewhere in the house, in the yard, or off doing things. Her husband is working on the car in the back. From time to time she hears the laughter and shouts of the neighbors' kids playing in a yard nearby. She is shelling fresh peas for dinner. The work is so familiar that she does it methodically, automatically, and without having to think about it. She takes the peas from the colander, separates peas from pods with a practiced movement of her hand, and drums the fresh peas into a bowl. She rocks slowly. Some moments she thinks of the things that need to be done in her yard: The grass needs cutting,

I'll have to remind Tommy, *and* Those nasturtiums are taking over everything, I think I'll pull them up and plant some geraniums.

Then she's a million miles away, remembering an event from her own childhood; My how I loved to do that, *she says to no one and to anyone. The mailman interrupts this reverie and she chats with him a few moments, catching up with his rounds, his arthritis, and the neighbors' comings and goings. The mailman leaves and she sees that among the four pieces of mail is a letter from her sister in Denver. She puts that letter on top and places the little stack of mail on the porch railing. She glances at the letter and looks forward to opening it. She wonders if it has some news about their brother's health and, as she thinks of him, she offers a quick prayer. When she finishes her work and washes her hands, she'll enjoy taking a few moments to read the letter. This whole scene takes maybe twenty minutes or a half hour.*

The banker is writing at his desk. His pen runs dry. He carefully blots the work that he has been doing and puts it aside. He reaches for his inkwell, unscrews the barrel of his pen, and dips it carefully into the inkwell. He engages the lever that will draw ink into the reservoir and pauses to allow the excess ink to spill back into the well. He then reaches into his drawer for a specially kept, small, soft, ink-stained piece of cloth and uses it to wipe the ink from the surface of his pen. He folds and replaces the cloth in the drawer, puts the two parts of the pen together, replaces the inkwell, and returns to his task. This whole scene takes maybe three or four minutes.

My point here is not to overvalue nostalgic tasks of days gone by, but to point out how far we've come from that leisurely pace and to call attention to what was going on in the minds and souls of these people as they lived these quiet moments of their lives.

As I wandered around my grandfather's farm, I was learning very important information, not only about my physical world—land, pigs, and tractors—but about who I was: "I'm with my grandfather today; he's my mother's father; he's from Ireland; he talks with a brogue; he loves horses and pigs. I think he likes to have me with him…" Of course these are not the words or the awareness that would have occurred to a ten-year-old boy, but you can be sure I was learning these things, and much more too.

The woman shelling peas has spent her time in a kind of contemplation. As she moved in her soul from her garden to her neighborhood to her childhood to her sister's letter, she too was learning important information about herself: who she is and what she wants. Even the mailman's interruption did not keep her from returning to her contemplation.

The banker refilling his dry pen sees a metaphor for himself as the busy executive: He is running dry, needing to dip into the well of soul, and he refills his reservoir of energy and patience.

These are all moments of Stopping. They are moments of remembering, awareness, and contemplation. My point is that these urgently important, life-giving moments that slow life down so that we don't miss the important parts are rare for us now. The good and hopeful news is that we can—and I believe must—make intentional choices to make them happen for ourselves. Because life no longer offers such pauses naturally, we can intentionally create times with little to do and of quiet work. We can place the seemingly blank spaces, the spaces that help us to learn important things, between the events of life.

Just as we have had to make specific choices to get sufficient physical exercise, so we now have to make choices to put spaces in our lives, spaces in which we have nothing to do. Creating these spaces is the purpose of Stopping.

Parents can help create safe but unstructured time for their kids, time with nothing to do but with adventurous spaces to do it in. You might not shell peas, but you probably wash dishes, cut vegetables, mow grass, or fold laundry. If you don't have a fountain pen to use as a metaphor for refilling your reservoir, you probably have a gas tank. The moments that naturally occur for us are probably not as quiet as they were in years gone by or as naturally conducive to contemplation, but that's not a problem. If we first are Stopped enough to notice them, we can change many of those moments from annoyances to life-enhancing opportunities.

Stopping ultimately has the same purpose of intentional living as American naturalist and poet Henry David Thoreau had in 1845 when he went to live at Walden Pond: "I went to the woods because I wanted to live deliberately, to front only the essential facts of life, and see if I could not learn what it had to teach, and not, when I came to die, discover that I had not lived." In the post-millennial era, most of us can't retire to the woods, so we have to create the Walden moments for ourselves.

CHAPTER 7
Stopping Before Everything

"Millions of persons long for immortality who do not know what to do with themselves on a rainy afternoon."

—Susan Ertz

Stopping is a gentle art and is like an encouraging word that urges us to make the right decisions and choices: the ones we really want and the ones that are life-giving. These decisions are both the big, life-changing ones such as a career change, starting or ending a marriage, or moving to a new home, as well as the smaller, day-to-day ones such as: *This purchase? That sales pitch at work? Tell her now or wait 'til later?* In both senses of the phrase, Stopping comes before everything: Stopping should chronologically precede everything we do as well as assume a position of priority in our lives.

This is no small adjustment for most of us. This is a change in direction that will affect all the aspects of our lives. But I am not afraid that clearly stating the magnitude of the change will prompt you to say, "This is asking for too great a change. I don't think I want to get into this." I am not afraid to tell the truth because the results are so promising: not only will you find more moment-to-moment peace, you will also find clarity in your life. Is there anything more important? And could there be anything much worse than knowing—when you are at the end of your life or even at the end of your day—that you missed it?

In both of my fields of work, ministry and counseling, I have had occasions to be with people as they are dying. At those moments, the saddest words to hear, and not the least common, are "If only I had known!" or "If only someone had told me!" The implication is that they would have lived their lives very differently and more in line with the truth they now see at the time of their death. And now, of course, they know it's too late. The realization brings a deep sadness.

This has led me to ask myself: Would they *really* have changed if they knew then what they know now? What if someone had revealed the truth to them? Would that have made a difference? My questions remain answerless until I direct them at myself: What do *I* need to know *now* so that I will not be in that situation? Since, as an adult, it is no one else's responsibility to tell me what I need to know, what is it that I must tell myself? These are questions that will be answered only in the stillness that allows the hearing of sometimes challenging truths and in the slowness that allows me to notice them.

This brings us to another point. It is so obvious that it often escapes our attention. It is this: slowness fosters remembering, and speed engenders forgetting. Czech novelist Milan Kundera makes this point eloquently in his novel *Slowness*. It is a point not only fundamental to the understanding of Stopping, but essential to living successfully in today's world. In Kundera's words: "There is a secret bond between slowness and memory, between speed and forgetting. Consider this utterly commonplace situation: a man is walking down the street. At a certain moment, he tries to recall something, but the recollection escapes him. Automatically, he slows down. Meanwhile, a person who wants to forget a disagreeable incident he has just lived through starts unconsciously to speed up his pace, as if he were trying to distance himself from a thing still too close to him in time."

Does that ring a bell with you like it did with me? Think of the times when you are trying to remember: you'll notice that you become very still and possibly stare into space. And when we want to forget something? Run, keep moving! Kundera states this truth in the form of equations: "The degree of slowness is directly proportional to the intensity of memory; the degree of speed is directly proportional to the intensity of forgetting."

The faster we go, the more we forget. Then what often happens next is that we forget that we have forgotten. What a state to be in! But when we Stop, we remember again and, therefore, find ourselves.

CHAPTER 8
Contemporary Contemplation

"If you can't meditate, vegetate."

—*Men's Health* **magazine**

Stopping is not meditation as it is generally understood. It is a practice intended for citizens of the post-millennial generation who have no time to stop and smell the roses or who haven't time or inclination to practice an elaborate system of daily meditation. It's for people who don't have time to fit in everything they are already obliged to do, never mind trying to fit in extras like sitting down and meditating twice a day. However, Stopping is in some ways a *variety* of meditation. It is what I call contemporary contemplation, designed for those too busy (or maybe moving too fast?) to formally sit and meditate; it's a way to care for the soul for those who wouldn't otherwise do it, even though they might really want to.

"Finding moments to engage in contemplative thinking has always been a challenge, since we're distractible."

—Nicholas Carr, American author

Stopping is specifically designed for people who are looking for a simple, uncomplicated, nondogmatic, yet effective way to cope with a too-busy life. While respecting and teaching many of the concepts and practices of Eastern (for example Buddhist) systems, Stopping embodies the cultural outlook and customs of the Western mind: it's brief, simple to learn, and effective.

From the time I first learned about meditation in my youth to well into the over-busy days of my adult life, formal meditation has been a challenge for me. It's not that I don't like it; I do. It's not that I have not done it; I have, for some periods of time, with success. I've also read many books on it. Certainly I know that when I do it, I benefit. It's just that I so often find my resistance to meditation stronger than my motivation. It's still hard to get it done. No doubt a simple case of the spirit is willing (but maybe not naturally inclined?) but the flesh is weak (or otherwise ill adapted?).

Stopping, because it is less structured, works better than meditation for me and for many of my clients, although the end results and some of the processes are almost the same. While I still occasionally meditate in a formal, somewhat structured way, I am always Stopping—many times a day, many more times a month, many, many more times a year. I don't find myself resisting Stopping as I do meditation. In fact, I look forward to it.

Perhaps it is a matter of personal preference. The words of Dr. Rachel Naomi Remen, a pioneer in training doctors in relationship-centered care, apply so well here: "I am not much of a meditator," she says in her book *Kitchen Table Wisdom*. "No matter. I have come to suspect that life itself may be a spiritual practice. The process of daily living seems able to refine the quality of our humanity over time." Yes. The intention of Stopping is to help us notice, enrich, and augment "the process of daily living."

What if our religion was each other?
If our practice was our life?
If prayer, our words?
What if the temple was the Earth?
If forests were our church?
If holy water—the rivers, lakes, and ocean?
What if meditation was our relationships?
If the teacher was life?
If wisdom was self-knowledge?
If love was the center of our being.
—Ganga White, yoga master

One of the purposes of any kind of contemplation is to awaken us, to help us to be in the present moment, so that in the moments ahead we will be on the right track. The word *contemplation* has Latin roots in words that indicate an intensive time spent in the temple to be aware of the signs and omens of the times. Contemplation prepares us for the present moment, and thus for whatever is next, and for what we need to notice now to enjoy success in whatever we are beginning.

I learned the hard way that if I undertook a self-improvement or spiritual project—anything from trying to lose a few pounds or quitting cigarettes to trying to be more patient with a difficult coworker or less angry and aggressive while driving in traffic—it was doomed to fail if I did not begin the project from a Stopped position. In this way, Stopping is a preparation for the challenges that face us at every turn and even the challenges that we propose and welcome.

The reason why so many of our well-intentioned projects fail is not from a lack of goodwill, not from a failure of willpower or determination, and not from a moral or character weakness. It's that we start these projects from a too-busy, distracted, and unfocused position. It's no wonder they often fail. So Stopping is a first step, a beginning, a prelude. It's the condition we need to be in so that our projects succeed. Beginners are welcome here.

A too-busy, distracted, and unfocused life also kills the power of imagination, an essential part of any healthy life. If we don't know or we cannot imagine what we dream or passionately desire, we will never be able to realize it. Stopping is a friend of imagination. During a time of Stopping, our imaginations are given space and encouragement to soar.

Stopping is also a primer for some of the more challenging spiritual books and systems that are offered today in such large numbers and various forms. Stopping allows you to be more receptive and positively critical and thus more successful in whatever you are attracted to adopt and practice.

Stopping can help you recognize a teacher when he or she appears and can help you to understand that all good teachers should respect your wisdom and not take themselves too seriously. In that vein, it seems appropriate for to me to say that if Stopping does not do for you what I am saying it can, if it does not bring you into contact with your important questions, and if it does not help you to become more awake and remember who you are and what you want, then, of course, you must leave it behind.

CHAPTER 9
Finding the Spaces between the Notes

"I am the rest between two notes..."

—Rainer Maria Rilke, poet

I believe poets are the ones among us who see most clearly. That's because they are always looking at life. Even though it may seem they are difficult to understand (just what does Walt Whitman mean when he says "I loafe and invite my soul"?), their vision, once felt, is the clearest we have. So you will find me quoting people like Frost and Rilke, Neruda and Angelou, and the ancients Horace and Cicero, because they are always looking at life, and looking leads to seeing what's there. Pierre Teilhard de Chardin, priest, paleontologist, and visionary, teaches that "the whole of life lies in the verb *seeing*." So my goal with the poets is to help us see what they see.

Poets are the visionaries I turn to when I need to find my way, when I need to see a true and unadorned reflection of myself, or when I need to learn useful skills for my journey. The German poet Rainer Maria Rilke was a passionate and intensely personal poet. In the following poem he gives beautiful expression to the meaning of Stopping. It is from his *Book of Hours* (translated by Robert Bly):

My life is not this steeply sloping hour,
in which you see me hurrying.
Much stands behind me;
I stand before it like a tree;
I am only one of my many mouths,
and at that, the one that will be
still the soonest.

I am the rest between two notes,
which are somehow always in discord
because Death's note wants to climb over—
but in the dark interval, reconciled,
they stay there trembling.

And the song goes on, beautiful.

What can we learn from this? In the first stanza, the poet tells us not to mistake his "hurrying," fast-moving life ("steeply sloping hour") for the authentic and deep life that is really his. No, his life is more, so much more, than that.

"Much stands behind me" represents all that he has to keep in his mind, to be aware of, and to remember, and "like a tree," he stands there and embraces it all. In the wonderful line "I am only one of my many mouths," the poet seems to ask us not to be fooled. Of all the things that he has said, only a few are really his. Of all the mouths from which he speaks, only one is authentic, and that one will be the first to be stilled. By death? By intimidation? By wisdom?

He is, he says, "the rest between two notes" of a song. Think of it. Think not of the beautiful, rich tones of the notes. Notes are what we hear, they are the wonderful things of our lives: the events and people. But "Death's note wants to climb over" or dominate, and thus the notes are "somehow always in discord."

Without the rest between, without the "dark interval" where values and meanings have their origins, the Death note would win. But it doesn't have to win. During the rest, life happens, value and meaning are given form, the soul deepens its reach, and the song is saved once again. And it goes on being saved again and again and again in all the pauses, long and short, of the song each of us is singing.

The poet asks that we do not define him as the rushing around that we see him doing, but that we should define him as the pause between the events to and from which we see him rushing, because it is precisely during the pause that the quality of the notes, and his true life, is born.

The poet asks us to be, like him, the rest between the notes: that brief, measured moment between the time when one note of the music stops and another begins. Without that rest, all would be chaotic racket. "Death"—that is distraction and forgetting—would dominate when all you fill your life with are the notes. All notes and no rests would be Babel. The sound would not be music; it would be more like a siren. But in the "reconciliation" of that "dark interval," the song "goes on, beautiful" because it's there that all the notes become organized and melodic. It is there that they take on meaning and give value.

"Music is the silence between the notes."
—Claude Debussy, composer

Here's a practical example of noticing the rests between the notes: You've jumped into your car after dropping off a package at the post office and are on your way to an appointment. You're thinking of what you just did or what you will soon have to do. Dropping off the package and your appointment are your "notes." You do those well. You are busy getting the notes right. But what you likely miss is the "right now," the in-between, the time between the notes, the time in the car or when you are going from one thing to another. That's the time I want you to notice. That's the time the poet calls valuable.

Pianist Artur Schnabel, agreeing with the Debussy quote above, in speaking of his music makes this point exactly: "The notes I handle no better than many pianists. But the pauses between the notes—ah, that is where art resides!" It is also where the art of living resides and where we transform discordant noise into the music of our lives.

Stopping is taking notice of the space between the notes. Stopping is making the space between the notes important. Stopping is transforming the space between the notes into life-giving alertness and remembering.

CHAPTER 10
Stopped: Awake and Remembering

"Beyond living and dreaming there is something more
important: waking up."

—Antonio Machado, poet (Translated by Robert Bly)

Picture a lone traveler on a journey, paused at a fork in the
road, considering the moment, fully awake, poised, not rushed,
aware of her power, and only when the time is right, choosing
the road and continuing the journey. A decision thus made
cannot be wrong. The journey will be successful, whatever its
outcome. The pilgrim is awake and mindful of the answers to
the important questions of life.

Now imagine another traveler stumbling down the road,
frantic with anxiety, unfocused, dropping things along the
way, unable to distinguish accurate directions from false ones,
tattered, exhausted, and, without thought, taking the fork in
the road that's the closest. Not an appealing model nor one we
would choose to imitate. Yet most of us do. Racing from thing
to thing or from note to note, in a frantic attempt to keep up or
to catch up, we lose our keys, our plane ticket, our cell phone,
ourselves.

Here is an example from my college years: It was my freshman year at Georgetown University. So taken up was I with the shouts of "revolt!" that I walked boldly out of class one day with hundreds of freshmen, practically our entire class. I have now forgotten what the intended revolt was about, some perceived inequality no doubt, but we were clearly serious. We had organized the revolt, kept it secret, and then screamed it to the world as we marched onto the football field, daring university officialdom to oppose us.

Then Joe Rock appeared out of nowhere. He was a 250-pound Jesuit priest—most of it belly—with a snarl calculated to induce terror and immediate submission into the heart of any fainthearted freshman. He lectured us for fifteen minutes with studied gesticulations and barely controlled roars. I can still hear his voice. "There will be no revolt! I'll give you three reasons why there will be no revolt!" Joe Rock always had three reasons for everything even though we were convinced he was thinking up the second and third as he was expounding the first. It was during his "three-reason" lecture that I remembered something: I was not a revolutionary and did not really want to be a revolutionary.

I had hit the ground running; I had begun this revolt without being awake or mindful. In no way was I Stopped. Neither, it seemed, were my cohorts. We were simply caught up in the heat of the moment. So Joe Rock's posturing easily worked. In fact, I was thinking during his lecture, "He's right, this is silly, this makes no sense at all…" Some revolutionary.

Mindfulness

Being awake—knowing who you are and paying attention to what is going on both inside and outside of you—is close to what the Eastern spiritual traditions call mindfulness. It involves being very present to this moment, to what you are now doing, to this feeling, and to this person in front of you. It is what newspaper columnist Adair Lara means when she recounts what her mother wanted on her birthday: "Presence not presents." It is noticing the tone of someone's voice and their body language, as well as noticing those things in yourself. It is seeing the many things that occur in your day and quickly establishing whether they are important or trivial. It is tuning in to other people and yourself. Being awake is a very in-the-moment act, an act of right now. It is the opposite of being distracted and unfocused.

Stopping brings you awake and to an awareness of the present moment. But it also helps you bring together the threads of your history, of your stories. It helps you to remember who you are, where you come from, where you are going, and where you want to go; to remember your original goals, ideals, and dreams; and to remember why you started doing what you do so that you can see if that's still what you want to do. Even if you have no clear answers for many of the big questions of life, it is vital to continue to remember what your questions are. Losing your questions is truly losing your way.

"My advice to you is not to inquire 'why?' or 'whither?' but just to enjoy your ice cream while it's on your plate."
—Thornton Wilder, American writer

Stopping is also remembering in a more literal sense: re-member-ing. That is, to collect again all the parts of you that have been left behind or scattered about in your hurry and to get all your "members" back again into a cohesive whole. The poet Robert Bly speaks of the "bag we drag behind us" as being full of those parts that we have lost the use of—our innocence, our spontaneity, or our playfulness, for example. Stopping is reclaiming those parts we did not want to lose, the parts that were stuffed in the bag, maybe years ago, and are hidden and forgotten.

These two gems, being awake and remembering, are another way to describe mindfulness and are the essential elements of Stopping.

CHAPTER 11

Stop and Go for It!

"Carpe diem!"

—Horace, *Odes*

Stopping is simple to understand. It's a period of time spent doing nothing in order to gain everything. It's taking enough time and creating enough quietude so that you can remember the important questions of your life as well as the current answers that you are bringing to them.

Stopping is a girl sitting in a sun-filled window seat gently stroking her purring cat, a woman with an open book in her lap gazing out the window and into a distant world, a man walking barefoot along an isolated beach feeling the wind in his face, a driver poised at a stoplight taking a deep breath and relaxing with a soothing thought rather than just wishing for the light to change, a busy nurse taking a one-minute breather and then smiling at her nasty patient, and a salesman mindfully eating his lunch while sitting on a park bench and looking at the sky.

Inherent in Stopping is the idea of creating enough space in your life, whether for thirty seconds or for thirty days, to make sure that you have first things first and that you are not so distracted that you lose the moments of meaning in life, whatever else you might be in the process of gaining.

Notice the definition of Stopping is "Doing nothing as much as possible." "Doing nothing" is a relative term here. Sometimes it will mean not doing much, doing something that takes very little energy, or doing something that you love to do. Paradoxically, doing nothing is doing something very beneficial. Again, Stopping should not be confused with inactivity; life is what it is about.

Stopping is not running from life or avoiding responsibilities. On the contrary, it is moving into life and its responsibilities in a new way. It is having the courage to go precisely where your meanings and values lie and spend time there. Stopping is like an embrace: it holds close and dear those moments which matter the most to you.

Carpe diem seems to be a perennially popular saying. I've seen it on T-shirts and mugs and it often makes its way into movies. *Carpe diem* means "Seize the day"; these are the words of Horace, a Roman poet who lived just before the change of the eras (65–8 BCE). *Carpe diem* is an encouragement to take advantage of the time you have. Contemporary equivalents might be "Follow your dreams," "Don't miss the chances life gives, you might not get any more," or "Take a risk." If you really want something, don't let anything get in the way. Have the guts to go for it!

Seize the day. Go for it. Follow your dreams. Take a risk. These encouragements to achieve and get things done were popular in the ancient times of Horace, and we are still quoting him. So what about Stopping in the face of *carpe diem?*—they seem to be at opposite ends of the spectrum. On the one hand we have "Stop, be quiet, take time to be spiritually awake, and remember the important things" and on the other we have "Seize the day, get out and go for it, get what you want, and do it now." Are these mutually exclusive encouragements? Not at all.

I would rather say they differ in sequence of application. In other words, before you seize anything, go for anything, dream, follow, or risk anything, you'd better know what it is you are seizing, going for, or risking. Because there is too much going on in our lives, we tend to be impulsive, to act before we think—or better—go before we stop. It's like the executive who was so busy climbing the corporate ladder that it was only near the top that the realization came: the ladder was leaning against the wrong wall. So before we get going, we had better start from a Stopped position or else our going, like my freshman revolt, will be inaccurately chosen, poorly carried out, unsuccessfully ended, or all three.

The combination of doing nothing and *carpe diem* is exactly what Stopping is all about. So with apologies to Horace, I say that we had better know what *diem* we want to *carpe* before we *carpe* it or we are likely to end up with the wrong day. Before you seize the day, stop for a day. Or even for a minute.

PART II
The Three Ways of Stopping

CHAPTER 12
Stillpoints, Stopovers, and Grinding Halts

"Finally it has penetrated my thick skull. This life—this moment—is no dress rehearsal. This is it!"

—F. Knebel, writer

Stopping has three levels. They are based on length of time: Stillpoints, Stopovers, and Grinding Halts. All are effective, but each one is meant for different moments of life.

A Stillpoint is Stopping quickly and doing nothing for just a moment. It is brief and meant to be used anytime, all the time, and many times a day. Stillpoints are essentially short: a few seconds, several minutes, up to a quarter hour or so. They are designed to take advantage of the unfilled moments in life: waiting for the microwave to heat your coffee, brushing your teeth, or sitting at a stoplight. They are also to be used at moments of stress: walking into an interview, when we feel anger, or when you know you're going to be late for an appointment. Stillpoints form the heart and soul of Stopping. They are its most common expression.

Somewhat less frequent are Stopovers, which are those times that are longer than a Stillpoint, say an hour or two to a couple days. These are the wonderful times of Stopping, when you really have the feeling that you have" been away" and have had a mini-vacation for the soul. A common expression of the Stopover is the quiet morning, afternoon, day, or weekend away, whether you go anywhere or not.

Grinding Halts will probably happen only a couple of times in most people's lives. They can last from a week to a month—or more. Obviously, these need more planning, require a larger and deeper commitment of time and energy, and typically happen at times of life transitions.

These are the three levels, or the three expressions, of Stopping. Of course the times for each are flexible. ("Am I doing a Stillpoint or a Stopover? Who cares! Makes no difference what you call it.") Each is effective in its own way, but the more frequent the repetitions or the longer the time, the more lasting the effect. Think of the three levels as going down (each one deeper and more effective) and plumbing the deeper recesses of your being, allowing you to creatively and enjoyably do nothing and to become more fully awake and recollected. These experiences will help you to make accurate decisions and to maintain your true life direction.

As the quote at the head of this chapter reminds us, what you are doing right now is not a dress rehearsal for your real life that will happen sometime later when you are more prepared. No, this is it! You are not waiting for anything to begin; you are already in the middle of it.

CHAPTER 13
Stillpoints: The Heart and Soul of Stopping

"Except for the point, the still point,
there would be no dance, and there is only the dance."

—T. S. Eliot, poet

Stillpoints are the expression of Stopping that can be used most often and that form the basis, or undergirding, of all Stopping. It is by far the most common use of Stopping. Stillpoints are short and focused. Creating Stillpoints during the day is fundamental to the incorporation of Stopping into one's life. They grow by accumulation and thus are the backbone that holds up the structure. A day with fifteen Stillpoints will make you much more peaceful, satisfied, and calm at the end of it, no matter how much you've had to do, how many people you've had to attend to, or how many fires you've had to put out. Stillpoints also bring you closer to joyful anticipation of the longer Stoppings.

The overwhelming advantage of Stillpoints—especially compared to meditation and other time-consuming systems of quieting—is that they can be incorporated into your life with minimal disruption and maximum effect. You can be with someone constantly for a whole day and that person would never know that during the day you had been renewed and refreshed by fifteen or twenty Stillpoints. I do it all the time:

As I am presenting a seminar to forty nurses, at least ten times during the presentation I do a Stillpoint. I take a deep breath, focus in, remind myself of what I want to create in this seminar and what I want to offer the participants, and then I go back to what I was doing. This takes a few seconds and the participants experience it only as a brief pause.

Stillpoints are life's little moments of gold that, when taken together, can give brilliance and joy to otherwise dull days. Stillpoints are the short times, brief interludes, quick respites, breaks, breathers, intermissions, and lulls.

But they are also intentional and are chosen for a specific purpose. They, as all Stopping, consist as much as possible of doing nothing and of stillness.

What you "do" during a Stillpoint is simple: You stop doing whatever you're doing, sit or stand, take a deep breath with your eyes open or closed, focus your attention inward, and remember what you need to remember. *Stop, breathe, and remember.* The remembering part is very flexible, it can mean recalling a belief or an event that motivates you. But it can also mean remembering a prayer for strength or peace, a message you need to hear at the moment like "You really enjoy this!" or a self-encouragement like "You can do it." Stop, breathe, and remember. Here are some examples of Stillpoints:

You are on the bus (or train or plane) and are staring ahead of you, perhaps focusing on the back of the seat in front of you. You begin by simply noticing your breathing for a few moments, then briefly bring to mind some of the people that are very important to you: parents, children, a spouse or partner, or friends. After a moment or two of this, simply smile, softly.

"Meditation [and Stopping] is the ultimate mobile device; you can use it anywhere, anytime, unobtrusively."
—Sharon Salzberg, Buddhist teacher

You are at the copy machine (or fax machine, or online, or in line) waiting for something to do what it is supposed to do. You relax your shoulder muscles, take a slow, deep breath with your eyes open or closed, and think of one thing for which you are thankful, for example: "It is really great that I have a friend like Chris."

The words from T. S. Eliot's poem at the beginning of the chapter are profoundly fitting for an understanding of Stillpoints. If it were not for the still point, there would be no dance. Dancing cannot continue indefinitely. There must be a point at which the dancing body stops, rests, no matter how briefly. It is that point and that time of stillness that gives energy to the dance, and the dance—life!—is all there is.

So, Stillpoints have a physical part (being still and breathing) and a spiritual part (remembering, praying, thankfulness, or other words that are good for you to hear). Sometimes the remembering part can simply be silence.

Simple, isn't it? The very essence of Stillpoints is deep, intentional breathing and a moment of quiet recollection. Since breathing is part of the essence of Stillpoints, this is a good time to learn the intentional breath.

CHAPTER 14
Breathing Is Inspiring

"I don't need to know how to breathe,' you're probably thinking. 'I've been doing it since the day I was born— without a single lesson. "

—Ian Jackson, writer

I'll never forget the moment I learned to breathe. No, it was not when the doctor slapped my bottom as a welcome into the world and I gulped my first intake of air. It was about forty-some years later when I was in training for certification as an interactive guided-image therapist. During one of the sessions, we were led through a breathing exercise. The woman leading the group spoke slowly, calmly, and clearly about the process of breathing and how many of us breathe shallowly.

That teaching changed my life. I don't think anyone around me was aware of it (or were they being polite and discreet?), but as I breathed several times deeply in and then completely exhaled, involving the entire internal mechanisms of a diaphragmatic breath, I broke into an instant sweat because the experience was so new and overwhelming. As I continued to breathe consciously and fully, I then began to shake just slightly, quietly, because the experience was so physically and emotionally revolutionary. I know it seems odd now (I must have actually breathed deeply before that?!), but it felt like my first breath and like I had never really breathed deeply before.

In the days and weeks that followed, I became a conscious breather, practicing frequently and learning the nuances of breathing.

Conscious breathing means to breathe deeply and intentionally. To breathe deeply is to begin the breath low in your belly and move it up into your chest.

To learn how to do this, begin by placing your left hand over your heart and your right hand over your belly button. As you breathe in, your right hand should move out and away from your body as your lungs fill with air, and your left hand should remain still. This movement should make you look "fatter" than you are; your stomach should be protruding. Then, as you breathe out, or exhale, your right hand should move back toward your body, and your left hand should remain still. The taking in of air moves your stomach, not your chest, out.

Too often what happens is that when we take in a deep breath, the left hand on the chest moves out, meaning that the air is kept shallow and high in the chest and does not bring oxygen to the lungs in an efficient way.

To take this a step further to an even more complete breath, begin with your hands placed as above: left hand on your chest and right hand on your belly button. Breathe in and watch your right hand move out. But this time, continue to breathe in and when the right hand is out as far as is comfortable, bring the inhale up to your chest and allow the left hand to move out also. Then, as you breathe out, or exhale, the reverse movement happens as your left hand moves close to the body first and the right hand follows. As you do these breaths in succession, you will see that there is an undulating motion as air moves from down to up and from up to down, from the stomach to the chest and from the chest to the stomach.

That's diaphragmatic breathing and it brings several profound benefits: It deepens your awareness of this particular moment and brings you directly into contact with the present. It internally massages the major internal organs, relaxing them, and creates a heightened awareness of yourself and, by its very nature, causes you to expand both spiritually and physically. *Spirit* and *breath* are from the same root, and *inspiration* means to breathe in. Breathing is inspiring.

How can I convince you of the power of a deep, intentional breath? Breathing is one of the involuntary activities of the human body, and it seems silly to practice or improve it. But the fact is that many of us breathe shallowly and, at times, particularly when stressed, we hold our breath so that we scarcely breathe at all. In order to experience the power of intentional breathing, begin by noticing how you breathe, when you hold your breath in and keep it tight (notice this especially when you are concentrating on something or trying to do detailed work) and how it feels when you do a deep, intentional breath.

A story from the Hebrew Scriptures applies here. Naaman was a powerful army general who became very ill. He consulted many wise physicians and healers, and none of them could restore his health. Word came to him from a servant girl that Elisha, a wise and powerful prophet in the neighboring country, could cure him. So, in desperation, Naaman and his retinue traveled to Elisha. When they found him, Naaman made his request that the prophet use his powers to heal him.

Elisha simply told Naaman to bathe seven times in the Jordan River and he would be healed. The general was infuriated. "We have rivers at home and I bathe in them every day and what possible good could come from simply bathing in a river! This is nonsense. We have wasted our time and effort." Naaman prepared to go. His servants, however, thinking that they had come all this way and that it would do no harm to try, convinced the reluctant general to bathe seven times in the Jordan River. He did so and was immediately cured of his illness.

Like Naaman, we tend to underestimate the power of something that is as ordinary as bathing in the river or breathing in air. Playing the role of Naaman, we might be tempted to say, "Breathing? I've been breathing since the day I was born, and I don't suppose I need to learn how to breathe at this point in my life. Besides, how can something so simple and everyday like breathing in and out really make any difference in my life?" I, as your servant, might say to you, "Well, Your Excellency, you've come all this way, it won't do any harm, and, who knows, it might make a difference. So humor me; why not just try it?"

For now, just trust in the benefits of deep breathing for your physical and emotional state, and, if necessary, just humor me a bit by trying it. Later, you will know for yourself. (If you're interested in this topic, look for James Nestor's book, *Breath: The New Science of a Lost Art.*)

CHAPTER 15
Stillpoints in a Turning World

"You must learn to be still in the midst of activity and to be vibrantly alive in repose."

—Indira Gandhi, Indian prime minister

You now have a clear idea of what Stillpoints are and you understand the intentional breath, which is their hallmark. Now you just have to begin to incorporate them into your everyday life. Here are some of the ways my clients and I have found to do that:

A Bathroom Breather

Yes, the bathroom is one of the best places to go (especially when you don't need to) to take a Stillpoint. "When everything gets frantic, everyone wanting something from me, I go to the bathroom," says Eddie, an office manager. "In my office, the bathroom has a lock, so I lock the door, look at myself in the mirror, and smile. Then I close my eyes, relax my body, take a few breaths, and spend maybe thirty seconds in quiet. I end with another smile at myself, maybe an affirmation like 'Take Care of Yourself,' splash some cool water on my ears, and go back to work. Total time lapse is two or three minutes. But what a difference it makes about how I feel about work!"

On a Scheduled Break

Cecilia, a receptionist, explains, "I take a small part of my break, at the beginning, and walk off a ways alone to take a few deep breaths and achieve a moment of quiet. Then I enjoy my tea with the others. The other day my girlfriend asked me what I was doing walking off like that. So I told her. She was so interested, she's trying it now." Sometimes you can use the whole break for this.

Walking from One Task to Another

"The hospital where I work is huge and I have to cover a large part of it several times a week," says Arnie, a physician. "I am generally alone. The walking is exercise but it is also a time for a Stillpoint, even though I'm moving. Conscious breathing and remembering what matters to me are what I like to do. It does make a difference, especially after a while. If I didn't do this intentionally, I would probably be worrying about what I had to do next or be distracted by my last encounter."

In a Tense Situation

Have you ever been in a difficult situation, when, for example, you are leading or attending a meeting and someone inappropriately raises his voice or says something mean, unfair, or vulgar? Chances are you tense up, hold your breath, wait for what will come next, and desperately search your brain for something that will fix the situation. After learning Stillpoints, Naomi took a different approach. She trains executives on issues of diversity in the workplace. One day, she faced a sudden, angry, and inappropriate outburst. "The very first thing I did was to remain quiet and take a deep breath," she says. "On the second breath, as I inhaled, I imagined the breath coming into me and bringing care, understanding, and love. And then, on exhaling, I directed the breath, with those same energies, through my eyes while I looked directly into the eyes of the man who made the outburst. The effect was immediate. The volatility of the situation was diffused, and the conflict could then be resolved later through a normal process."

Notice that in this Stillpoint, the power was in Naomi. It can be in you, too. You can breathe *in* what you need and breathe it *out* where it is needed. The words that Naomi imagined during the second breath were "care, understanding, and love." In the exhalation, the effect of the words was disarming and powerful. You can do this at home when you are about to explode at your child or spouse or after they have exploded at you. As this example shows, Stillpoints are not only a healthy way of taking care of yourself; they also enable you to treat others better.

When You Feel Stuck

Try this the next time you are having trouble with some task. Close your eyes for a moment and imagine inhaling the energies of concentration and relaxation. Then open your eyes and, as you breathe out, direct the power of your breath into the task at hand. Repeat this process to build a cycle of moving energy.

Commuting

Often when I am speaking to a group on Stopping, a participant's first personal connection with the idea will be the time spent commuting twice a day. "I call it 'decompression time,' " said one man as he told us what he does to make the transition from work to home. "My commute lasts anywhere from twenty to forty-five minutes, depending on traffic. As soon as I get in my car, my transforming begins. I loosen my shirt, put on a relaxing tape—don't listen to the news—and do everything possible to think of my home and my family: how my wife has spent her day and what the kids might be doing. When I finally get there, I move much more easily into the very different world of home."

At the Computer

Often, we wait for the computer to do something and find ourselves alternately staring at the screen and looking around with an impatient/bored attitude. A perfect time for Stopping. Close your eyes, breathe, remember why you are doing what you are doing. Open your eyes while breathing steadily, and, for as long as it takes for the computer to do what it's doing, itemize the things you are grateful for. Time ordinarily lost to frustration is now changed to increased peace.

The Power of a Stillpoint

There are several things you can do to enhance the power of a Stillpoint. You can add a simple, short, self-dialogue or affirmation at the beginning or end of your Stillpoint. Some examples are: "I'm okay, I can handle this," "This will be over soon, probably in a few hours, and I can deal with anything for a few hours," or "This evening I will take care of myself with a nice _____."

Another good enhancement is to ask, "What would_____ (fill in the name of someone, dead or alive, personally known or not, whom you admire) do in this situation?" Then imagine that you are receiving her or his energy right now, and breathe it into you. Another tool is to visualize the difficult situation you are facing: Close your eyes and "see" it in your mind's eye. In your visualization you make everything go just as you want it to. The rehearsal can lead you in the real situation. Many competitive athletes will attest to the effectiveness of this rehearsal visualization.

Please don't underestimate the power of a Stillpoint of even a few seconds. A glance heavenward takes maybe a second and a half, but for you at this time, it can be full of meaning and power because you have already determined its meaning and power. For example, if you are a person of faith, you can say to yourself, "As I glance at the sky (or even at the ceiling), I remember the divine presence in my life and that grace is available here and now."

A gesture that is hardly noticed by those around you can empower you in the same way. Here is one I use when I am in a stressful or uncomfortable situation: by simply bringing my thumb and index finger together to make a circle, I remind myself that "This too shall pass." For me it brings comfort, courage, and perspective. Why? Because it immediately sends me to my deeper self, my inner life.

The examples above show how Stopping is not simply a system, it is also an art. It leaves so much room for you to make it your own, to bring your personal style and creativity to the process. The more you use your creativity to imprint Stillpoints with you own uniqueness, the more effective they will be.

Stillpoints can also be a bit longer: the fifteen minutes you spend in the doctor's waiting room, the twenty-minute bus ride, the half hour driving to your appointment, and so forth.

The moments of Stillpoints are endless. Search your imagination for yours or for ways in which you need them. These are the times that most accurately correspond to the poet's image of the "rest between the notes." Think of the events of your day as the notes in a song. For the music to be melodious, so that it doesn't sound like a siren, you need to put the pauses in place. During the pause of a Stillpoint, the goal is a period of quiet, of "doing nothing," of being aware of who you are, and of what you want. Then your song "goes on, beautiful."

CHAPTER 16
Stopovers: More of a Good Thing

"Spend the afternoon. You can't take it with you."

—Annie Dillard, author

While Stillpoints are the most common way of Stopping, the real challenge for most of us is the next deepest level: Stopovers. These are the longer times spent doing nothing: an hour or several hours, a day, a weekend, or several days. This is the gourmet fare of the Stopping feast. Even though they are longer in duration, Stopovers are still at the speed of light because they must take place within the context of our fast and full lives.

It is sometimes easier to take a longer time away from work less frequently than it is to take shorter times off more frequently. For most of us, it is more likely that we will take a full day off every two months or so for a Stopover than that we will take an hour every day for, say, meditation. Both are good. It's just a question of which you will actually do.

Think of Stopovers as those stations on a long, leisurely train journey where you get off and look around, enjoy the scenery, breathe the fresh air, and return to your journey feeling rested and as if you've experienced a change.

Stopovers involve getting away for a while and they have a happy effect: you'll feel renewed and ready to go again. Jon Kabat-Zinn, a renowned specialist on meditation and stress management, says, "The stopping actually makes the going more vivid, richer, more textured. It helps keep all the things we worry about and feel inadequate about in perspective. It gives us guidance."

One of the necessities of the profession for any family counselor—maybe for your work too—is to be able to maintain the balance of caring deeply about what is happening in your clients' lives without carrying their pain into your own life. An hour-long Stopover is often my way to do this. Sometimes it will happen naturally during the day, otherwise I will schedule an hour to be a space between the notes of my clients. I walk mostly, though sometimes I go to a cafe and, accompanied by a cup of tea, watch people.

"My work is very intense," said a woman who supervises a large health care facility. "At work I am always 'on,' and when I get home I need time to adjust to this totally different place of family life. So I have a very strict rule: I get to be alone for a half hour before anyone gets any of my time. I think this would be my major Stopping of the day. It's taken a lot of work to make the kids see why I need it, but gradually they have understood."

Stopovers are important for everyone. For most of us, to take a significant amount of time for this purpose, our motivation and determination must be strong and clear. Remember the ultimate purpose: to wake up to what is going on in your life, to keep first things first, to remember who you are, and who you want to become, and to remember your ultimate values and meanings. Who can *not* afford Stopovers?

"All of humanity's problems stem from man's inability to sit quietly in a room alone." —Blaise Pascal, philosopher

Perhaps the best way for many of us to first experience a Stopover—a longer time away doing nothing—is to block out a period of time ahead of time—a morning, an afternoon, or even a whole day, maybe a month from now in order to give yourself some time to get used to the idea. Mark it on a calendar, perhaps plan an overnight for yourself. Allow the doing nothing part to feel positive to you: "There is really nothing I have to do for this whole time. No pressure and no expectations at all."

Practically speaking, many Stopovers happen during vacation time. If you vacation with your family, perhaps you could arrange to have a day to yourself and for another member of the family to do the same. On its own, time off from work is not necessarily Stopping. In fact, many seem to cram their vacation so full and so fast that it defeats the purpose of rest and renewal. So consider doing a Stopover during vacation or even a whole Stopping vacation. It just might be your best vacation ever.

CHAPTER 17
Stopovers on the Way

"[Going on retreat] has something to do with an aspect within each one of us...unknown to science...that longs to be at peace."

—David A. Cooper, author

The experiences presented here are real Stopovers by real people. The stories were gathered in conversations by phone, letter, and email. They were shared by people who had either read about my work on Stopping or attended one of my seminars. As you can see, people have been generous in sharing their experiences:

A Structured Weekend Retreat

"I generally don't like most organized retreats," said Barry G. in a phone conversation, "but that was before I discovered a silent, directed retreat. I believe that is what you are calling Stopovers. I was apprehensive as I went for the weekend, all that time with nothing planned and so few people there. A friend had encouraged me to do this when I told him I was often disappointed in retreats, but I was getting cold feet as I arrived. Well, I needn't have. It was wonderful. I can't recommend it enough. I do it now every year because if I don't, I seem to mix things up and have a hard time keeping straight all the things that are going on around me, especially with my family."

Your Own Weekend Retreat

You don't have to have a retreat center. One young woman, Janet, rented a small, inexpensive motel-type unit in a rural community close to some hiking trails. She spent a weekend alone, roving the hills, eating simply, and resting a lot. "As I think back on it now," Janet said, "I see that it was what you are describing as a Stopover. Of course I didn't think of it that way then. I just did it. I do remember that I didn't tell people what I was doing. I think I would have expected them to think me odd."

On a Bus

A long-retired schoolteacher, Howard L., in his eighties took a three-day bus trip to visit his daughter. He wrote to me: "I didn't plan for this to be a Stopover, but when I read about Stopping in your article, I realized that was exactly what I had done. It was so different. I hardly talked to anyone on the bus, but just remembered a lot of moments and made sure that the few I have left are spent in the right way."

A Nighttime Reverie

Pam is a nurse. She wrote about her "life-changing Stopping" after attending one of my stress clinics. She spoke of her hospital work in these terms: "Everyone was under a lot of stress and there was a feeling of insecurity and anger. I felt the symptoms of burnout: I dreaded going to work, on my days off I would be thinking about work and not enjoying the day, and, worst of all, I would snap at my husband and my one-and-a-half-year-old son. I thought to myself, 'if I am not able to handle this, then I must be a failure.' I was at my breaking point. So, I decided to Stop."

One night, very late, after she returned home from the night shift, she "had had enough! After a good cry I sat at our kitchen table and asked myself 'What is really important to me? What makes me happy?' " Thus passed the hours of Pam's long night, alone at her kitchen table with her questions, the pause between her notes, her dark interval, her Stopover.

And with the dawn? "My number one priority was to be the best mother, and number two was to be a supportive, caring, and understanding wife. Family was more important to me than work. This sounds kind of corny but, in a way, I felt that I had a kind of spiritual awakening that night."

Her Stopover brought about practical changes, too: she put in for a transfer and took a month off to visit her mother, sister, and other family members in Japan. Finally she added, "I hate to think of what I might be like now if I didn't stop that night."

Just Staying Home

The busy, type-A executive editor of a small publishing house found that her way of doing a Stopover was to stay put. "Twice now, I have taken a week off and just stayed home—no calls, no visitors, and no going places. I slept a lot, read a little, 'did nothing,' and worked silently in the garden." This is sometimes called a "staycation."

A Spontaneous Opportunity

Soon after she had heard about Stopping, Beatrice, a woman in her forties, called me to say that her Stopover had caught her unaware. "All of a sudden," she said, "I had an appointment canceled and a whole afternoon with absolutely nothing planned. The kids were in school, my husband was out of town, it was a beautiful day, and I had about four hours. Right to the coast I went, to my favorite isolated beach, almost without thinking about it. Like I knew I needed to do this. I was in another space for those hours, and things, at least later in retrospect, became clearer for me."

A Birthday Gift to Yourself

Gerald Reid told of his Stopover in the newspaper. For his birthday, Reid told his wife that he just wanted to spend the day with her and Nathan, their thirteen-year-old son. He wanted them all to do nothing. "But Dad, it's your sixtieth birthday!" his son protested. "You don't even want a present?" "No," responded Reid. He just wanted to spend the whole day completely and exclusively with the two of them. After some resistance from his wife and son, they began to go along with it. His son got into the idea by wishing him "Happy Nothingday, Dad! What do you *not* want today?" They played games (a concession by his wife who doesn't like games), she cooked what he liked, and they talked to each other. He received cards from both of them with messages of love. "Are you going to do nothing next year too, Dad?" his son asked him before bed. Reid asked him why. "Oh, nothing is more fun than I thought it would be," he answered.

A Day Off for Rest and Rejuvenation

A recent issue of *Men's Health* magazine featured an article titled "I Want to Be Alone." Executive editor Joe Kita suggested a day alone filled with healthy pleasures. He acknowledges to his readers that "to spend a day alone, tending to nothing but yourself, probably sounds foreign and even a little shameful." His day's retreat includes silence, hiking, simple food, a nap, exercise, a hot shower, and getting to bed early.

The Power of a Stopover

These stories show that Stopovers cover a wide variety of experiences, from an hour to several days, from a planned event to a response to one of life's challenges, from a quiet time of insight to a life-changing decision, from a bus ride to a retreat house, and from going someplace different to staying home.

This is a good place to mention the expectations or the hoped-for results you might have of your Stopping experiences, especially of the longer Stopovers. What I want to encourage is that you leave that part open ended. Like my Stopping experience on the North coast, I became aware of the results and implications only gradually, not all at once or suddenly. To have too-specific expectations is often to be disappointed. Part of the gift of Stopping is the gradual discovery of what you were previously unaware of. The ideal attitude to take with you on your Stopover is: "Let's see what happens." What all Stopovers have in common, at their conclusion, is a more generally awake and aware you.

CHAPTER 18
This Is Your Body Talking

"Prevention is better than cure."

—**Erasmus, theologian and philosopher**

Of course, all of us have probably done Stopovers many times in our lives. But instead of the Stopovers being a conscious choice, they were the result of getting sick. Sickness is often the body's way of talking to us and of getting us to stop when our minds and hearts are so overwhelmed by the challenge of too much that they can no longer get the job done. Not all sickness is of this sort, of course, but too much of it is. A sickness-induced Stopover is the body's way of saying, "If you're not going to stop yourself, I will have to force you to stop."

Sicknesses are an ineffective way to experience Stopovers. Because you're feeling sick, it's difficult to pay attention and appreciate anything. You're not in a receptive state of mind or expecting any kind of positive goals, and you just lie there feeling awful and waiting for it to be over so you can rise and run again.

I have a friend, Harry, who works long hours and takes little time for himself. One would call him driven. About three times a year he gets sick—the flu or a bad cold—and has to spend a week in bed, hardly capable even of talking or reading, and then he's back to overdrive. Sickness serves him as an enforced Stopover. But it is a detrimental way to do it: He misses most of the benefits and—more importantly—enjoys none of the pleasure. He only achieves the minimal bodily needs for survival. My hunch is that if he took the same amount of time that he spent sick, one week twice a year, and used it for a scheduled Stopover, he would not only get sick less often but enjoy life more.

Our bodies speak to us in many different ways. Learning to read your body's language before you become sick is an important result of the cumulative effects of Stopping. You will notice the patterns of sicknesses and identify the various parts of your body that pain you.

Stopping encourages you to ask body questions: What is this backache telling me? (Am I "carrying" something I don't want or need to carry?) Why am I always getting a sore throat and cough? (Do I want to voice something that gets stuck in my throat?) Answers to these kinds of questions—even the questions themselves—come in the silence of Stopping, which allows us to notice our current state of health and thus attend to it and prevent possible ills.

CHAPTER 19
Excuses, Excuses!

"An excuse is worse and more terrible than a lie; for an
excuse is a lie guarded."

—Alexander Pope, writer and poet

To incorporate Stopovers consciously into one's life rather
than getting sick is no easy task. It takes determination, clear
motivation, and grit because Stopovers involve a significant
amount of time. The excuses for not taking the time for
Stopovers are endless: too much to do this afternoon; too
long away from a spouse, family, job, or sick relative; or too
expensive. Excuses are examples of the problem of too much
described in part I.

But if you are like me, your biggest fear is yourself. That's what
loomed up for me before one of my Stopover experiences,
a week's silent retreat. Questions plagued my imagination:
What if I find that I am as weak as I fear? What if I remember
something horrible that happened to me many years ago? What
if—worst of all—as I turn my gaze inward, I find nothing of
value there, or nothing much at all? Then what?

The trick in facing my fears was not to avoid these questions
but to ask, literally, "Okay, then what? What if I *do* find trouble
or even nothing at all when I am Stopped?" "Well," I thought,
"then I had better know it now and see what I can do about it

rather than miss something that needed attention." If I needed help, it would be easier to get help now than to wait until I might be too old, or too tired and unmotivated. But more than anything, I did not want to miss something vital in the experience of human existence. I wanted to live my life to the fullest, and if there was anything in the way of my becoming all I could be, I needed to know.

It turned out that my retreat was plagued by distractions, chief among them a friend who happened to be in the hospital close by the retreat house and who was recovering from major surgery. Perhaps four times during the week, I went to visit him at the hospital—a serious infraction of the retreat's parameters. So, in the middle of it, I just sort of wrote off the retreat as a good try and let it go, perhaps unconsciously thinking that my worst fears wouldn't even have a chance and I could blame my avoidance on something else—visiting my sick friend. Then, when I was least expecting it, the last two days of the retreat I experienced some of the deepest spiritual moments of my life to that point.

The image that came to me as I was facing my fearful questions before that silent retreat was an image that was given birth during my high school years: me as a sixty-five-year-old man waking up too early one cold, gray morning and knowing in my deepest soul that I had missed what I most wanted. When I was sixteen, I don't think I could have told you what it was that I most wanted, but I did know that it was urgently vital and that, for me, it was somehow spiritual.

If fears of facing yourself are there for you as you contemplate the possibility of Stopovers, then you are like me and like almost all of us. These fears are natural. I will talk about working with these fears in much more detail in part IV. For now, know that they can be faced—and overcome.

Anyone who incorporates Stopovers into his or her life has given priority to life as a spiritual adventure. If you are reading these words at fifty-something years of age or older, please remember what sixteen-year-olds cannot know: it is literally never too late. Now is the best time to discover who you are and what matters the most to you. .

Can you think of a Stopover as an expression of love and an act of kindness to yourself? Indeed it is. But if being loving to yourself is not a good enough reason for you, consider this: a Stopover is an act of generosity for others in your life and for the world at large. A composed and focused soul is a deep richness for all the world, a great gift for those who encounter you, and a desperately needed example in this off-kilter and polarized world.

Often the most difficult part of the two-way street of love is the direction that comes toward you. That is, we tend to focus on the giving of kindness and neglect the reality that we also need to receive it. A Stopped person can notice and appreciate the generosities that come his or her way; a rushed, harried, and stressed person cannot. And because love is a two-way street, others observe your qualities of equanimity, calm, and peace, and it gives them not only an example but also permission to explore the same path.

There is a social deterrent to Stopovers. Taking time away from your daily life and responsibilities—whether for an hour, a day, or a week—and, especially, telling people that you are doing it, seems a very unusual or dramatic thing to do and an act which is perhaps more attention-getting than you are used to. It could cause people to talk: from your friends, "How can she leave her family for so long? I wish I could do that," "He must have a lot of money to be away from work so long," or "She's on some kind of retreat? Seems foolish to me, I wonder if she has a drinking problem"; from your kids, "Mom, you're going to be away all that time? Who will cook?" or "Dad, are you feeling all right? Maybe you should just see the doctor"; and from your parents, "Seems like a foolish waste of time, you should be trying to get a better job."

How long should your Stopover be? To get to your answer, follow this recipe: Combine the state of your being, the realistic amount of time you can actually get off, and what you actually feeling like doing at the time, and shake them together until the answer presents itself to you. Generally speaking, the longer the better.

Stopovers almost always involve a sacrifice—always of time, sometimes of money—but like any valuable sacrifice, there is good achieved. In this case, the achievement is making sure your whole life is on the course you want it to be on. Not a bad accomplishment for a morning's—or a day's—time.

CHAPTER 20
The Watersheds and Sea Changes of Life

"Never swap horses crossing a stream."

—American proverb

Stillpoints and Stopovers are advantageous for everyone and can be incorporated into life on a day-to-day and week-to-week basis. A Grinding Halt is different. It's an extended time that happens much less frequently, perhaps once or a few times in a lifetime, and may not be needed by everyone. This is not to say that a Grinding Halt is not possible or very beneficial for most of us.

Generally, a Grinding Halt marks a significant life transition or decision, or possibly a crisis. This transition can be termed a watershed, symbolizing a turning point that makes everything flow to a different system, or a sea change, indicating some deep and all-pervasive, but slower, shift of emphasis that has profound and long-lasting effects.

Some Grinding Halts are not optional: for example a serious illness or a pandemic. I am writing these words during the worldwide coronavirus pandemic, or Covid-19. Most of the world's people are experiencing a type of Grinding Halt named sheltering in place or quarantine. (See the next chapter for a fuller treatment of these types of Grinding Halt.)

My crisis in the ministry was also a time when a Grinding Halt was needed. My old life made no sense anymore, and I had no idea what the next step should be. Frequently, Grinding Halts are associated with a midlife crisis because the call to such a transition often comes at midlife, when the pull of spirit is strong.

"Is this all there is to life?" is the question I asked myself before that first and most significant Grinding Halt of my life. The Grinding Halt was the occasion by which I was able to know that I could indeed accomplish something that seemed at the time beyond my capacity: leaving the ministry as a way of life.

At age forty, I found myself pastor of a large parish in Boise. I loved Idaho and had been happily working there since my ordination in 1963. Suddenly, my midlife crisis hit with a wallop. I was no longer happy or fulfilled by my work. What used to mean a lot to me no longer did, and the positive feelings I valued in the past had changed into doubt and confusion. Even leading the Sunday worship services with the parish no longer touched me as it did.

My first coping technique was avoidance. I ran from the parish and school responsibilities, trying to get others to take my place. I became quite good at racquetball and surrounded my daily game with an hour of preparation and an hour of cooling down. This was very different behavior for me. Up to this point, I had been a hard and enthusiastic worker, bordering from time to time on becoming a workaholic. Now I was running from my truth.

My question, "Is this all there is to life?" implied that there must be some other areas of my life that I needed to explore. It was a clear indication to me that the values and meanings of my life to this point no longer moved me as they did. More than anything, that is what scared me. At the same time there were other questions: "Is this merely a stage in my growth?" and "Is this the time for me to stick it out and buckle down when the going gets tough?" Some wise people advised me in that direction.

I was plagued by questions that brought up anxiety, guilt, and fear of loss and of what I might discover: Do I value the life to which I have committed myself? Does it have meaning for me? Even if it doesn't, have I not promised to live it perpetually? Why am I feeling so isolated now when even a year ago I was not? What is best for me to do?

I needed to stop. So I did. I was fortunate that I could; not everyone can do it as easily. I had a conversation with my well-respected bishop during which he finally asked me, "Dave, are you asking me or telling me that you are going away?" I thought I was asking him; he recognized that I was telling him. If I had to name the force that allowed me to face these questions, I would call it emotional aching over the loss of meaning.

I spent my Grinding Halt, a month, in an isolated town on the Northern California coast taking painting classes for an hour a day, which was for me a totally new way to do nothing. That's all I did. For the most part, I just kept to myself. My questions, which now were not so demanding, faded into the background. I felt like my internal computer was scanning all my files, moments, facts, and feelings of my existence up to that point and that this scanning was going on all the time as part of my autonomic nervous system; it was out of my conscious control.

The purpose of the scanning was to ensure I didn't forget any necessary element as I made a possibly life-changing decision. The quiet was to assure that I was not too distracted by life for the scanning to take place. In the meantime, what I was externally doing was trying to mix pigments to capture the unique green of the cypresses found on the California coast and creating a beginner's bunch of watercolor paintings of that stunning and scenic coast.

By the end of my stay, the internal scanning was finished. I returned to my responsibilities for one year, at the end of which I made my decision. I left my position, returned to school, earned my degree and psychotherapy license, and began a new life as a family therapist. This, indeed, was a watershed moment: a dividing line that will continue to serve as a major point of transition in the course of my life.

As I reflect on this experience, I realize that my Grinding Halt would not have been possible—I just would not have had the power to get it done—without having in some way, years before, incorporated what I now call Stillpoints into my life. It was the accumulation of those moments that gave me the courage to do what I had to do at that moment of pressure and that moral crunch. It was a life-changing decision that involved disappointing a lot of people, breaking vows that I had taken, and violating long-standing family rules, as well as taking a risk to find out if I could personally carry it off and make it in the world.

"The quieter you become, The more you are able to hear."
—Rumi, poet

I can't say that my transition was without problems, regrets, or pain. I can say that I know it would have been much worse—more messy and more hurtful to myself and others—without the Grinding Halt. I can also say that at every stage of the transition, I had a sense that I was at least minimally aware of all the elements that were in play for me. And it has been a happy decision, thanks to Stopping.

During major transitions, the influence of the spiritual is a strong, almost magnetic force, because these major changes always involve our values and meanings of life. In the course of the change we are rightly concerned that we may lose them. Soon after I left the ministry, a thoughtful woman in my parish sent me a small card which, sadly, I have misplaced over the years. But I remember clearly the idea of the words on the card: Don't lose the ideals that have safely brought you this far. Receiving it was one of life's little gifts. I hope one day I will be browsing a long-unopened volume and will come upon her card.

What are your watershed moments? What are the sea changes in the ocean of your life? Are you in one now? Is one looming on the horizon? Maybe it's time for a Grinding Halt. And, if not now, chances are that there will be one sometime in your future.

CHAPTER 21

Grinding Halts Are Good for You

"No retreat. No retreat. They must conquer or die who've no retreat."

—John Gay, author

The need for Grinding Halts indicates that something big is going on. They are often needed, as in my case, to avoid some undesired result. As the epigraph above indicates, if we do not have a way to retreat or to get away for a while in order to allow some as-yet-unavailable idea or power to present itself, the only possibilities seem to be waging war or death. Grinding Halts give us the productive time to arrive at a healthy alternative. Here are several examples of the ways that a Grinding Halt may happen:

Time Alone in the Mountains

Jeffrey is a graduate student in his late twenties with teaching-assistant duties, a serious girlfriend, and part-time work. "Frazzled, totally stressed out," he described himself at the time. "I had very little money and absolutely no time at all." But he did have "two large decisions" facing him "involving love and work." He also had an old car, some camping equipment, and a strong desire to be awake spiritually.

He put together a Grinding Halt for himself that took some coordinating but was worth the work. He planned it around spring break, spent a few months saving money for missed work, and got the encouragement of his girlfriend ("She thought it was a great idea," he said, "she knew I needed it.") He spent twelve days at a secluded campground, living in his tent.

"I read my sacred writings, hiked, kept notes, cooked on my camp stove, and changed my life," he said. "When I'm sixty, I'll forget a lot about these years, but I know I'll always remember that time alone in the mountains."

A Nine-Day Retreat

Sally is a married woman in her mid-thirties, a mother of two, a part-time teacher, and a frequent volunteer at her church. She decided that life had become overwhelming. It wasn't that she was particularly unhappy—in fact her life was on the surface very satisfactory—but she was "becoming emotionally numb, not really giving attention to what I wanted to give attention, and even when I did, it was like I was someone else doing it. I felt a stage removed from myself."

Her Grinding Halt took the form of nine days of silence and quiet at a retreat facility just a few miles from her home. Her biggest challenge was her husband and friends. She took the time and energy to explain what was going on and how important this was for her well-being and her family. Reluctant at first, her husband supported her and later did his own form of Stopping. Her friends came around only after she had returned.

"One friend still thinks it's a bit silly, that it's fine if you're old and retired and have nothing else to do," Sally says, "but now, I don't care if people don't like it. I know how important it is for me. I can't wait to do it again, maybe in a few years, and for an even longer time."

"It's difficult to explain exactly what I got out of it," she said, "but I can say that I felt more confident that I knew myself better, that I had somehow strengthened my relationship with God, and that whatever I did from now on, I would not feel so isolated or abstracted from life."

Sally's experience came at a moment of spiritual crisis and at a turning point in her life. Notice her major transition was not a dramatic rupture of life events nor an emotional upheaval. This was a sea change kind of transition: slower and quieter.

Epidemic, Quarantine

I mentioned above that I write these words as the world is experiencing the unwanted and largely unprepared for Grinding Halt of sheltering in place or quarantine caused by the coronavirus, Covid-19. It will undoubtedly become a watershed in contemporary history.

The title of this chapter might seem inaccurate in the face of such an unpleasant and restrictive Grinding Halt, for indeed it is home to everything from inconvenience to catastrophe, from annoyance to death. However, in the long run, for the people who survive it is, like foul tasting medicine, good for you: it allows the virus to come under control, for survival to happen.

During such an enforced confinement, here are some points to consider:

- In addition to making sure that all are as safe as possible, make a decision to take care of yourself and your family emotionally and spiritually; the pressure and stress of a confinement can be significant.

- Practice intentionality and mindfulness—that is, try to be as awake as possible to the present moment. Ask, for example, "Once this is over, how do I want to look back on my response to this event?" Then proceed accordingly. Perhaps within this longer Stopping (Grinding Halt) you can practice the shorter versions of Stillpoints and Stopovers. Watch for opportunities.

- A Grinding Halt is always a time for taking stock, checking to see that your priorities and your behaviors are the way you want them.

- The event will probably be a watershed, a dividing line in the lives of all: before and after the pandemic. Ask yourself, do you want to return to what was "normal" before this event? Is that possible? Desirable? Think about those questions during the event.

An Island Sojourn

Here is a personal experience. Several years ago, in the spring and after months of planning, I rented a simple, one-room cabin on Lopez Island in the middle of Puget Sound off the coast of Washington. I arranged this trip so that everyone knew well ahead of time that I would be gone and that only emergencies would justify a phone call. I brought only one book and a journal. I had a bicycle and sufficient food for myself. I walked a lot, bicycled, read a little, wrote a little, meditated twice a day, and spent most of the day basically supporting life and doing nothing—just being. I rarely talked to anyone and, for a few days, spoke to no one at all. For two weeks, I just was.

I chose this way to do a Grinding Halt for several reasons. I had already done a week-long silent retreat and wanted something different and longer. Also, I felt drawn to that part of the world and to life on an island in a remote setting. It was a place where my soul felt at home.

I did it at that time because it was a moment of transition in my life and I wanted to be as awake as I could be so that I would make the right decision. Should I leave the social service agency where I was working as a family counselor and take the leap into private practice? Many of my old doubts came back to plague me: Could I do it? Wouldn't it be safer and wiser to stay with something secure but limited rather than go out and take a risk?

Once back from the island, my confidence seemed to take over and I opted for the risk. My transition succeeded. Would it have done so without a Grinding Halt?

To answer that, let me again use the computer as a metaphor. As I understand it—and it's probably not a technically accurate metaphor—a computer constantly scans numerous bits of information, all in the form of a series of ones and zeros, and gathers only what it needs to do the requested task. That's what happens during a time of a Grinding Halt. Your internal computer scans your life, all that has gone before, all the paths you have trod, all the teachings you have received, and all your values and meanings of life. The hallmark of the Grinding Halt is the acts of noticing these things, counting them, and saying to them, "Yes, I have noted you. I am aware of you. I have taken you into account as I make my decisions for the future." Some of this scanning is quite conscious and deliberate, but most of it is unconscious and automatic. It happens as you ride your bike, cook your meals, and gaze at the sea.

Around the World

Ann had worked her way up to marketing director in a small company. She had graduated from a prestigious college and through mentoring, native intelligence, and experience had gained wisdom that was at least equal to a graduate degree. She was doing very well. Then, just like that, she quit. She spent three months traveling the world, working as she went, to "get in touch with herself." When she returned, she got work as a marketing director for one of the biggest companies in her field. Her Grinding Halt brought her clarity and, ultimately, a better position.

Canceled Workshop

Susan tells of her unexpected experience of a three-week Grinding Halt. "The instructor became ill and a long-anticipated resident writing workshop was canceled at the last minute. I was on a small island—a mile by a mile and a half—off the coast of Maine, so I just stayed there. At the time I was mad at my boyfriend who went to Europe without me, so it was a weird context. But what happened for me is that the power of nature took over. It was incredible.

"I was by myself, and yet I was with nature." She wandered the island and visited the many artists there, looking at their work. "I noticed the weather change, from cloudy to cold to sunny. My body rhythms and the rhythms of nature became my clocks."As with many, Susan's Grinding Halt led her to appreciate the natural world. Think for a moment of what she did: three weeks essentially alone while wandering around a small island and being aware of the changes and rhythms, subtle and dramatic, of the natural world—a significant achievement.

Illness and Death

Sometimes Stopping is in response to a life event that is overwhelming. Barbara is a fifty-nine-year-old woman who had been married thirty-seven years and had one child, a thirty-five-year-old married daughter. She wrote to me, "Three years ago my husband, Jerry, became quite ill and, after five miserable months of doctors and tests, was found to be HIV positive. Three days later he was hospitalized with PCP (Pneumocystis carinii pneumonia)—an AIDS diagnosis. Five days after that, I found I was also HIV positive. Jerry recovered slowly from the pneumonia only to fall ill again and again until he died a year and a half ago."

Soon after her husband's diagnosis and after several attempts to find an appropriate counselor, she found an understanding and helpful priest. "I remember saying to him at my first visit that I wanted more but I really couldn't say what it was I wanted more of! My future seemed to open before me like a black abyss—and I was very much afraid." She decided to do something about it.

"My husband's religious tradition has rather elaborate funeral services including a forty-day memorial service. Right after that, I retreated. I closed myself off from as much of the world as possible. My daughter brought me groceries. I went nowhere but church. Six weeks after his death, family and friends began to get on with their lives, and I was left to my own devices, as it were. During this time, I was not lonely. I had plenty of time to read, ponder, mind-wander, meditate, experience, and work through various stages of grief and pain.

"Surprisingly, what came out of all this was the most marvelous enlightenment of one very pure, simple fact: God loves me unconditionally! My whole life had changed. My focus was crystal clear.

"I firmly believe if I had not had this opportunity of Stopping when I did, this great revelation, this enormous gift would not have come into my life. I was able to open myself to it not even consciously knowing what I was doing or why. How long has this been going on inside my soul?

"Now I feel my life is just beginning. Wonderful things have happened, and doors have opened."

So, what are you wondering about Grinding Halts? Are you drawn to the idea? Or maybe you are put off by it? Perhaps just somewhat neutral? Maybe you have, in fact, already done a Grinding Halt. If you are drawn to do one, then things will take care of themselves and you probably will do one. If you are put off or neutral toward the idea, my request is only that you remain open so that if you become aware of the need for a Grinding Halt, you won't miss it. You'll recognize what you need and be able to respond.

CHAPTER 22
Growing "Like Corn in the Night"

<hr>

"The way to do is to be."

—Lao Tzu, philosopher

Just how does Stopping work—whether Stillpoints, Stopovers, or Grinding Halts? Earlier I used the metaphor of a computer and the internal scanning that it does. When we are Stopped, the scanning happens on its own; we give ourselves time—create an opening—for anything that needs attention on some level of our consciousness. The fascinating thing about the process is that it does not have to be conscious. You don't have to analyze your way out of anything. All you have to do is put some space and time around yourself, and your marvelous mind and soul will sort it out, because now you have the conditions,—silence, solitude, and no noisy distractions—for your always-present inner wisdom to be heard.

Henry David Thoreau has another, more earthy image to show us how we grow during Stopping. Here are his words from Walden, which could well be described as the key American document from the 1840s, to support the Stopping I am encouraging a hundred and eighty years later.

First, he describes one of the wonderful moments of his two-year experiment of living alone at Walden Pond in Massachusetts in order to "live deliberately" and awake:

> I sat in my sunny doorway from sunrise till noon, rapt in a reverie, amidst the pines and hickories and sumachs, in undisturbed solitude and stillness, while the birds sang around or flitted noiseless through the house, until by the sun falling in at my west window…I was reminded of the lapse of time.

This is a wonderful description of a contemplative kind of Stopover: "from sunrise till noon, rapt in a reverie." Then he tells us how he grew.

> I grew in those seasons like corn in the night, and they were far better than any work of the hands would have been. They were not time subtracted from my life, but so much over and above my usual allowance…I minded not how the hours went…it was morning, and lo, now it is evening and nothing memorable is accomplished…I silently smiled at my incessant good fortune.

"Like corn in the night" is a wonderful image that is full of power. Can you place yourself inside a cornstalk on a moonless night? Can you imagine being inside the growing ear, absorbing the nutrients from the earth, having retained in your flesh the warmth of the day's blazing sun, drinking in the moisture of the dew, and combining it all to create the miracle of the bright, yellow food?

That's how we grow when we're Stopped. It happens on its own, we don't have to *do* anything.

CHAPTER 23
Freeing and Finding Your Truth

"To search out the deep truth of life, to lift a veil from its fascinating secrets..."

—Maria Montessori, educator

I hope that by now you see that Stopping—in all its forms—works because it allows for and facilitates truth, your truth, to have its way. In fact Stopping can't fail; it can't be wrong because there is nothing to be wrong or right about—no content, no doctrines, no dogma, no beliefs, and no system of adherence—only a clearing away of whatever is cluttering up your truth. And when your truth is freed, identified, and given wings, your life will be enhanced, deepened, and enriched. Stopping is a way, a very simple way, to get to your truth.

I want to encourage the freeing of the truth that is most essentially *you*, the identification and answering of *your* calling, because I believe that is the most important accomplishment in life, and that is how you most clearly discover and develop the values and meanings of your life.

What you encounter while Stopping will be unique to you. It is also noble, worthy, and life enhancing, even though it can bring to consciousness painful or difficult issues. The most significant fact is—oh, what a different world it would be if we all believed this truth!—there is nothing wrong with you. An important goal of Stopping is coming to know that fact, not hoping that it might be true, not thinking that it is sometimes true, but knowing, on many different levels, that there is nothing wrong with you: through knowledge, facts, and feelings in your mind, in your body, in your heart, and in your soul. And this is true even though you, like all the rest of us, can think of many areas where you need improvement, times when you are less than wonderful and even moments when you are downright terrible. Those are things that show that you are human, that you are not God.

But Stopping also involves another dimension of encountering truth, one that balances and fulfills the process of freeing. It is *finding* our truth. By that I mean the need to get out of our own way, to get over ourselves, to go out from ourselves, and to find that *something else* that adds a special dimension to life.

The ultimate goal in finding truth is discovering one's purpose or calling. They are blessed who know, at least to some degree, the primary reason for their existence and the answers to questions like "Why am I here?" But equally blessed—if not more so—are those who are aware of the questions and are attentively searching for the answers, even if their attainment is ultimately illusive. It is precisely in the searching that our nobility lies. Stopping's purpose is to serve the search.

So Stopping can't go wrong even if it brings challenges and messes. Much more likely is that it will be the projects and plans you undertake before you are ready to undertake them and the search for purpose that lead you far in the wrong direction because you are inattentive: you are not Stopped.

When you are actively engaged in both processes, freeing your truth and finding your truth, then life—no matter its current state—is right.

CHAPTER 24
Everyday Spirituality

"We must find some spiritual basis for living, else we die."

—Bill Wilson, AA founder

At this point it is evident that Stopping is essentially a spiritual process. *Spirituality* is a challenging word. Many folks don't like it because it is too general, bland, and loaded with so many meanings that it can end up meaning nothing. Ernest Kurtz and Katherine Ketcham ask, "What is spirituality?" in their book *Spirituality of Imperfection.* They say that "to have the answer is to have misunderstood the question," precisely because it can mean so many different things. While acknowledging this problem, I have been unable to find a satisfactory substitute for the word. So rather than throw it out, I have formed a broad, working definition based on a description by theologian David Griffin and on an idea from psychologist James Hillman:

"Spirituality is the ultimate meanings and values by which we live our lives, both on the peaks and in the vales."

That is, spirituality consists of what we sacrifice for, what we put first, and what we would let go of last. It is our answers to the big questions of life, and it is our deathbed truths. It is the meanings and values that influence how we live from day to day, from decade to decade, and for a lifetime. Our morality is based on our spirituality; the rightness or wrongness of how we understand our actions is based on what we value and where we find meaning.

I like to call this definition *everyday spirituality* because it is useful for and accessible for literally everyone, all the time: for those within a system of religious belief with very otherworldly values, as well as for those who are not associated with such a system and who might hold very worldly values, or any combination of the two. This allows a wide range, from the strict orthodoxy of an ancient, organized religion to a personally created system that involves such practices as music, reading, exercise, and volunteerism and any combination thereof, or none of the above. Grace knows no bounds. For those with the eyes to see, everything is sacred.

The second part of the definition, "living on the peaks and in the vales," has to do with the use of the words *soul* and *spirit*, and I can think of no better way to understand their differences than by using the "peaks and vales" metaphor of Jungian psychologist, James Hillman.

"Spirituality is the ultimate meanings and values by which we live our lives, both on the peaks and in the vales."

Hillman identifies *soul* as residing in the vales, the low, fertile valleys of human experience. "Soul is always tethered to life in the world," says psychologist and author Thomas Moore, commenting on Hillman's idea. "It can't be separated from the body, from family, from the immediate context, from mortality." Soul is sometimes messy and dark. Soul is what grounds us in the world. It gives warmth and moisture to life and to our meaningful relationships with other people.

Spirit, on the other hand, tends "to transcend these limitations of the valley," notes Moore. Spirit focuses on the "afterlife, cosmic issues, idealistic values and hopes." It resides in the higher, drier, and more airy peaks in the sky. Its focus is transcendence—clearing the limits of the body and the other darker, messier tendencies of human nature.

But—and here is the point I want to emphasize—when the spiritual transcends the earthiness of the soulful to the point where it becomes split off from the soul and receives no influence from it, the resulting spirituality readily "falls into extremes of literalism and destructive fanaticism," as Moore notes. So a spirituality that separates spirit from soul will lead to only half the truth, to serious one-sidedness, and to deep trouble.

When I use the words "spirit," "spiritual," and "spirituality," I include both the peaks (transcendent and selfless aspirations) and the valleys (earthly struggles of delight, confusions, and muddling through); both the crisp, silent, clarity of a moment of isolated and absorbed contemplation and the experience of intense erotic pleasure with your beloved; both the isolated monk disciplining his human nature in order to achieve a higher union with God and the mother who, with love and humor, handles way too many messes in the valley of family life.

I shall never forget a hallowed moment in my life that included both spirit and soul. I was sixteen and was on a canoe trip with a dozen other kids and our guides in the lake-studded wilderness of northern Ontario. We had made camp early that day and chores were done. It was the time between evening and night which at those northern latitudes is so blessed with a unique and amazing light. I took a canoe out on the lake, alone.

For some reason I stopped (yes, Stopped) in the middle of the lake and lay down in the bottom of the canoe and kept very still. I heard (I can hear it now!) the water gently lapping at the sides of the boat, the faint, occasional sounds of my fellow campers talking and laughing far in the distance, and the silly laugh of a loon at the other end of the lake. I saw only blue-gray-rose sky. I felt the coolness of the water against my back through the canvas skin of the canoe as well as the hardness of the canoe's wooden ribs. At that moment I knew something utterly important—even though it is still challenging to put it into words. It was something like: everything is right and I am part of it. I feel profound gratitude for that moment.

As is often the case, that transcendent peak was quickly transformed into a messy valley. I paddled quietly back, and, as I was arriving at our campsite, the guide began to yell at me, "Never do that! That is a very stupid thing to do! You should know better!" What appeared to be an empty canoe in the middle of a lake, he explained to me, is an immediate alarm signal for anyone seeing it. Of course, I knew right away what he meant. He saw me leave and, at some point, he happened to look out and saw only what appeared to be an empty canoe and no me. But I hadn't thought of that.

A moment on the peak, a lesson in the valley; both are necessary and holy.

The other point to remember about spirituality is that we all are spiritual whether or not we are religious or call ourselves spiritual, whether atheist or believer. We all have values and meanings by which we live our lives, in the valleys and on the peaks, whether they are examined or ignored. In this sense, spirituality is like health. We all have health, well or ill, attended or neglected. So with spirituality. The important question is not whether we have a spirituality or not but whether our spirituality is leading us to integration, knowledge, and wholeness or not.

===

"Whether you believe in God or not does not matter so much.... You must lead a good life. And a good life does not mean just good food, good clothes, good shelter. These are not sufficient. A good motivation is what is needed: compassion without dogmatism, without complicated philosophy; just understanding that others are human brothers and sisters and respecting their rights and human dignity."
—Dalai Lama XIV

===

Often spirituality and religion are confused. Religion is the form or structure which at its best fosters and feeds human spirituality and at its worst kills it. Spirituality, however, is a process of maturation toward the fulfillment of your meanings and values, which lives outside as well as inside religion.

I believe it is helpful for everyone to have a specific spiritual practice, even if only loosely identified and very personal: that is, a way composed of specific teachers, events, rituals, moments, habits, customs, readings, sayings, doings, works of service, traditions, celebrations, icons, works of art, artistic expressions, places, spaces, times, symbols, words, images, sounds, colors, acts of kindness, and so on, almost endlessly, or any number of these in any combination.

Having a spiritual practice is helpful for at least two reasons. First, it acknowledges that you are living both on the peaks and in the valleys and that you have the desire and appreciation not only for the peaks but also the humility, humor, and practical skills for the valleys. Having a practice encourages your spirituality to be useful; it supports an everyday spirituality.

And second, because it will help you in your Stopping. Stopping is essentially spiritual—that is, it deals with meanings and values. If you have a spiritual practice or a specific religious belief as you cultivate Stopping into a habit, you will be simply adding another dimension to your practice.

Imagine having an important insight about yourself, maybe a new way of seeing that you are more seriously dedicated to serving the needs of people than you previously realized or that you are more deeply passionate about learning to play the cello than even you suspected. Now imagine not knowing what to do with these insights that are the spiritual gifts of Stopping. With a spiritual practice in place, you can go to your readings, your prayers, your sacraments, your trusted guide, your service work, your music, or whatever makes up your practice and use it to process the gifts and, therefore, as a way that leads you to integration. Thus, the gifts of Stopping are not lost or missed, but developed and enjoyed.

With Stopping, I want to access your deeply felt desires to feel less stress, to make better decisions, to be a better parent, friend, coworker, or spouse, to feel more organized and efficient, and especially to experience joy. No, that's not quite right. What I really want is to lead *you* to access those same desires of your heart. I want *you* to access the desires that are too often blocked and frustrated by poverty—of pocketbook and spirit—by fear, or even by the churches and institutions that should be their very connectors.

I believe all deep and yearning desire is in some way a wish for integration and unity with the world and, ultimately, with God, or however you define the divine or ultimate reality. From elegant corporate boardrooms to raucous and mean streets, there is not much difference in the aching desires in the hearts of people. Even the addictive cover-ups of these desires are similar—money, power, cocaine, alcohol, crime, violence, apathy, and boredom—although the styles are often different. Beneath these painful expressions is an often hidden but noble and gracious yearning.

Stopping is designed to connect you to your heart's desire and to help you identify it, name it, pursue it, and realize it. It does this by giving you the opportunity to be quiet enough, often enough, to hear your own wisdom. In fact, it isn't really the Stopping that will do it; it is you. Stopping can help you get to the point where you recognize your own wonders.

PART III
The Gifts of Stopping

CHAPTER 25
Stopping's Benefits

"The only thing that keeps us from floating off with the wind is our stories. They give us a name and put us in a place, allow us to keep on touching."

—Tom Spanbauer, author

Our Stories

One of the primary benefits of Stopping is that it allows you to notice and keep all the stories of your life. These, perhaps more than anything, will lead you to your truths. Stories are a "connection to our roots, to where we come from. Through stories we can understand our lives," says Joe Bruchac, storyteller and writer. Storytelling is "almost like calling the gods. A powerful spiritual presence makes itself felt, and one can be quite literally swept away by it."

But we often miss the stories that are ours and that come to us from our ancestors, because, adds storyteller Laura Simms, "modern life, with all its noise and distractions, makes these stories difficult to hear." Stopping prepares us to hear them.

Bruno Bettelheim, child psychologist and educator, saw fairy tales as medicine for the soul. The fairy tale is therapeutic "because the patient finds his *own* solutions, through contemplating what the story seems to imply about him and his inner conflicts." Clarissa Pinkola Estés also sees the healing power of stories. She too compares stories to medicine: "The flow of images in stories is [a] medicine [that] acts like an antibiotic that finds the source of the infection and concentrates there. The story helps make that part of the psyche clear and strong again."

"We don't need lists of rights and wrongs, tables of do's and don'ts: we need books, time, and silence. *Thou shalt not* is soon forgotten, but *Once upon a time* lasts forever."
—Phillip Pullman, author

Is your child out of sorts? Perhaps you can find her medicine in a storybook. Try to pick one out that will speak to his heart. And you? When are you out of sorts? What story do you need? A Stillpoint might bring you just the right one, perhaps one you had not remembered for a long time, from a book or from your life or one you had not thought of as a story.

One way to look at all of life is to see it as one story after another and as stories that we are telling both to ourselves and to everyone else. For example, try The Story of Yesterday— your yesterday. Begin it with something like, "I awoke way too early, I think it was about five o'clock, and began to think about my project..." continue through, "Then just after a quick lunch I ran into Harvey who I hadn't seen in months. We spent ten minutes catching up and decided..." and end, perhaps, with, "I finally flopped into bed at eleven and dreamed that I was..."

World's Needs

From the intimacy of our personal stories to sweeping issues of the whole wide world, at any given time in history, there are certain priorities that the whole world seems to need to understand and develop. Stopping can also help us be aware of these and add whatever we can—be it a rich and powerful contribution or simply our little part.

For example, one of the worldwide issues that it seems to me we all need to be aware of as I am writing this is the changes that the world's climate is experiencing. Stopping at its best can help us in our roles as world citizens.

It is a natural outcome of Stopping to gain a heightened awareness of one's surroundings, both close in and far away. It is an inevitable result; one begins to notice more and more. This leads, by a natural progression, to an examination of the relationship between Stopping and environmental awareness, both locally and globally. Thus, the most passionate heart of Stopping is a deep forest green.

Naturalist Bill McKibben understands Stopping. I know this from reading his introduction and annotations to a fine edition of Thoreau's *Walden*. He describes a one-week backpack trip, beginning with the challenge of the noise of internal chatter, through the time when the "chatter in [his] head began to subside," and up to the point, at nightfall, when he was watching a blue heron and "the sky blackened, the stars spread across the sky bright and insistent; we were unimaginably small, this heron and I, and extremely *right*." These are the words of someone who notices and especially of someone who cares. Stopping leads to caring.

And caring invariably leads to questions. From McKibben's reading of *Walden,* Thoreau—whom he wonderfully describes, capturing his peculiarly American spirit, as a "Buddha with a receipt from the hardware store"—poses two essential questions for our times. The first question stands as an "assault on the Information Age," on computers and all the fast systems of communicating: "How can I hear my own heart?" The second, which I believe flows from the first, is addressed to all of us who make up the consumer society: "How much is enough?" Is constant growth the best for us all? The illness of the Age of Anxiety—cancer—offers us a valuable and provocative symbol for our times: cancer is uncontrolled growth.

"When one tugs at a single thing in nature, one finds it attached to the rest of the world."
—John Muir, naturalist

These two questions, "How can I hear my own heart?" and "How much is enough?" are wonderful examples of the kinds of questions that we can look at, understand, get a feel for, develop a sense of, and, especially, care about and maybe even begin to answer through our ongoing practice of Stopping.

Stopping's Gifts

In addition to these benefits there are many other gifts of Stopping. It is somewhat like living in a wonderful old mansion for many years and then one day discovering a whole new wing with new rooms full of wonderful things. We are that big old house, and we have some wonderful rooms waiting for discovery and exploration.

Like the rooms in the mansion, the gifts of Stopping have always been there, but we've perhaps been too distracted, too preoccupied to explore them. Fully discovering the beneficial gifts of Stopping is like walking through the newly discovered wing, opening each of the doors, and spending some time in the rooms.

I have tried to choose the most important of Stopping's gifts to look at, the benefits that get most closely to its heart. Surely there are more; every Stopping experience will be proof of that. But these six seem to be essential:

The capacity for paying *Attention*; achieving true *Relaxation*; knowing and enjoying *Solitude*; forming strong but flexible *Boundaries*; embracing your *Shadow*; and identifying and living out your *Purpose*.

These are the gifts that Stopping offers those who embrace it. They are gifts that are sometimes discovered for the first time, but more often are rediscovered after being lost or misplaced and are frequently already present and in need of appreciation. Stopping develops and encourages these gifts into new levels of excellence and enjoyment.

Let's look at each gift—one by one—along with some suggestions for how to encourage them.

CHAPTER 26
The Gift of Attention

"Someone sold us out—but only when we ceased to pay attention."

—Timothy Findley, Canadian author

Being awake and remembering is paying attention. With this gift, we are encouraged to notice what is within us, what is important to us, and what is attractive to us. As Stillpoints are the heart and soul of Stopping, so paying attention is the heart and soul of all the gifts of Stopping: it forms its very soul and nothing gets more directly to its heart. It is the trait that defines the Stopped person as aware of what is going on right now and remembering all that's important and meaningful.

Distractions are the enemy of attention. Many of us are so busy, so overwhelmed, and thus so spiritually asleep that any given day can consist of mindlessly moving from one distraction to another. In such a day, it is possible never once to be really awake or to know and feel why you are doing this routine over and over or even if you really want to do it. Or maybe your whole day is spent focused on others: your kids, spouse, customers, clients, or boss. Time for yourself is squeezed in, hardly remembered, and haphazard. Losing track of the time and date is a sign of distractedness.

In such a state we are simply moved by whatever happens to be loudest or most demanding at the moment. Not that our pursuits are without importance or value, but if we are not present to them or aware of what we are doing or why we are doing them, at least to a degree, then we are distracted.

By distraction, I also mean anything that takes your mind or soul attention off what it wants to be on. Distractions are often trivial and demand your attention as if they were important or meaningful. This causes you to put last things first or the cart before the horse. Literally, you're off track, you're dis-tracked.

"The Internet is designed to be an interruption system, a machine geared to dividing attention.... We willingly accept the loss of concentration and focus, the division of our attention and the fragmentation of our thoughts in return for...the information we receive."
—Nicholas Carr, author

Anything that tells a lie about itself in order to get your attention is also a distraction. Some advertising is a great example of distraction. The ad says, "This is important, this is true," and it often makes these statements about precisely what is *not* important and *not* true. It often lies, and, perhaps even more amazingly, it insults us by assuming that we are not aware that it is lying. We have grown accustomed to it, which makes it even more powerful.

Listen to these comments: "Make a more wonderful you" by using this soap; "Be at the top" by buying this car; and "Life is worth" this brand of crystal. As if soap could make you more wonderful or driving any kind of car would put you on the top of anything worthwhile. If we are attentive, we have knowledge of our wonders, of what we want to be on top of and of what is worthy in life. If we are not attentive, we could have the tragic fate of being guided through life by the advertisers of Madison Avenue.

Just yesterday I heard on the radio that wearing a particular brand of eyeglasses "will tell the world who you are." No, it won't.

Dis-tracked, we pay attention to what is not life giving, helpful, healthy, enjoyable, nor important, while we hope whatever we are focused on will be all those things for us. Distracted, we miss the important moments. They pass us by and we don't even notice: a phone call from an old friend, a momentary view of the rising full moon through the dark trees, a remark or a question from a child, or the light and color of an autumn evening—all missed, untapped, unused, and lost. Nor do we even notice that we did not notice.

It is difficult to categorize distractions because almost anything can become a distraction and almost anything can be made noble. It has to do with being awake. An attentive person can say to a distraction, "You are a lie and I give you no importance and no influence in my life." The key question is always, "What is really going on here? What is the truth of this situation?"

Picture a person who goes from a sterile marriage to boring work, goes back home to an evening of stultifying television, and starts all over again the next day. A sad existence. However, a person with a *different attitude*, a person who is constantly *paying attention*, who also is married, who works at a job, and who watches evening television can have a life that is richly meaningful. We must tell ourselves constantly: "Wake Up! Pay attention! What is really going on here?"

Stopping allows us to pay the necessary attention in order to prioritize life. In this way, Stopping is something like the death of someone we know. It leads us to value and appreciate every moment of our own existence as priceless and irreplaceable. At that moment we often ask the long questions and the big questions: "Am I doing what I really want to do?" and "Am I being who I really want to be?"

That was my challenge years ago when a friend died of AIDS. I have been filled with so many feelings from the moment he told me of his illness to the moment I am writing this: anger; empathy; appreciation for his good example, friendship, and engaging sense of humor; frustration at not being able to do anything; and so many more feelings.

But what ultimately came out of my experience was the determination to be attentive to my life. His death reminded me in a very intimate way that life is short, often difficult, unpredictable, of limitless value, and has parts that are important to me and others that are not. So I should get it all in order right now. Tomorrow? Who can count on that?

Forgetting follows directly from distraction. We forget where we came from, how we came from there, where we are going, and why we are going there. We forget our values and the rituals that ground us and tell us who we are.

When we are inattentive, we can also forget what is truly valuable. We all enjoy getting a new piece of sporting gear or a new gadget for the kitchen. But in the long run, a new tennis racket and a new blender probably mean nothing really important. A tennis racket can bring you some pleasure and perhaps help your game; it cannot make *you* better or happier. It's an easy slide from "the prestige of ownership" to believing that you are now more fulfilled and are somehow better.

However, to keep balance, we must not miss the beautiful soulfulness of the things of the world. The same tennis racket and blender can indeed help bring to our lives valuable qualities that enhance our moments both on the peaks and in the valleys. As always, it's a question of balance and of meaning and value.

"Patterns of attention—what we choose to notice and what we do not—are how we render reality for ourselves, and thus have a direct bearing on what we feel is possible at any given time."
—Jenny Odell, *How to Do Nothing*

When we are distracted and forget what is true and important for us, we tend to make mistakes. I forget appointments, I bring the wrong book to the meeting, or I know the correct size of the battery I need but I buy the wrong one. When we go without Stopping, the chances of making a mistake along the way are high.

When I think of paying attention, I think of the words of Sister Mary Odilo, my seventh-grade teacher. She would say to me (too often), "David, stop daydreaming and pay attention!" She was right, of course; I did have to learn mathematics. But I—and every other kid sitting in a schoolroom and daydreaming on a spring afternoon—was also right; there was a lot of important stuff I *was* paying attention to as I was daydreaming. The trick is to hit the balance between daydreaming and passing the math test.

Being attentive is about noticing. I really like the word *noticing*. It implies so much. It has a lack of urgency and a quietness about it. When we notice things or moments, we take them in, consider them, and note them. They become ours, not in a grabbing kind of way but in a friendly and useful way. As I reflect on this past week, I *notice* some moments: a very small girl, seated in a grocery cart, looked right into my eyes and said, "My mommy gots a new toofbrush!"; I had a dream last night of a lion and a lioness; a call to a friend in Canada was, by chance, right during her fortieth birthday celebration; the weather Tuesday began cold and cloudy with high scudding fog, but by noon it was warm and sunny; and I spent some time with an old friend I had not seen for a while and we had good, animated conversation.

All these are just little moments in my life, a few out of hundreds and thousands, just as in your life. Why notice them? They remind you, they form you, they deepen your soul, they help put things in the right order, they connect you to the world, and they keep you awake. And on top of all that, they can bring you pleasure.

CHAPTER 27
The Gift of Relaxation

"Health requires this relaxation, this aimless life. This life in the present."

—Henry David Thoreau, essayist

Relaxation is the gift of achieving physical and mental ease in your body, in your dwelling, in your country, and in the world. It is knowing that you belong and where you belong. Without a minimum amount of true relaxation, we undertake any endeavor from a disadvantaged basis. Humans simply were not made to stay in a state of stress all the time.

Over the centuries, our bodies have changed very little while our culture has changed dramatically. When the hormones that trigger the fight-or-flight response were coursing through the body of the caveman, he was almost always facing a physical stressor: he either killed the woolly mammoth or was killed by it. For us humans now, most stress is not physical but psychological or spiritual. If you get an unfair evaluation at work because of the petty jealousy of your supervisor, what can you do? Fight (which means confronting the supervisor or other authorities, even though you know you'll lose) or flight (which means quitting your job and starting over.)? Most often we can do neither. Both responses are unsatisfactory.

But our bodies were made to do one or the other and the hormones continue coursing through our veins on that mission. That negative stress energy has to go somewhere and do something. *It does not go away on its own.* Most often, what it does is attack its host: you. You get sick, irritable, have backaches, shoulder aches, flu, colds, get fat or thin; whatever form your stress takes. That is, unless you do something about it.

I believe many people today have seldom known real relaxation and thus all their projects begin with a handicap. Perhaps they have lived with so much tension and stress from childhood that they are unaware of what they are carrying and it feels normal to them. That's a serious problem. Learning how to relax is crucial to our physical and emotional well-being.

I use the term *relaxation* both in its ordinary sense, what we all mean when we say we feel relaxed, and in a slightly more clinical sense, the return of a person to normal equilibrium, or balance, after a period of stress. In other words, once you have experienced stress in your life, you need to do something with that negative stress energy to balance the time of stress with an opposite time of being relaxed. You can't just return to normal without a relaxation time and expect to have real recovery from the stress. Remember, the negative stress energy does not go away by itself; it accumulates and, if not balanced by a time of relaxation, continues to do you harm. Understanding this is key to true relaxation.

Response to Stress

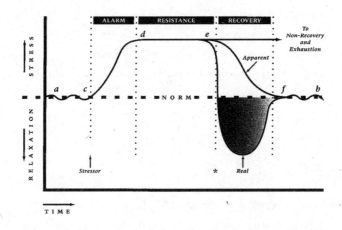

Use this diagram to picture it graphically: The dotted line begins on the left with point *a* and ends on the right with point *b*; this is your normal lifeline. Above the line you are in stress territory and below the line you are in relaxation territory. You begin at point *a* and travel toward point *b*. A little way along, a stressor occurs (point *c*)—say someone recklessly cuts in front of you in traffic, nearly causing a serious accident and scaring you enough to make your heart pound and your muscles tighten from a rush of adrenaline. That stress event moves you up through the initial alarm stage (*c* to *d*) and above the line well into stress territory. It would be common for one to feel the stress from this event for days or even weeks after. The resistance stage (*d* to *e*) is the time you spend coping with the stress. It can last from a few moments to years, depending on the degree of stress

Now here's the important point: If you merely return to your normal lifeline at point e and continue on your way, you have not fully recovered from the stress. You still carry the effects of the stress though you might not be aware of it; it accumulates with others that are already there. For real recovery, you must go below the line into relaxation territory for a time and then return back up to the line of normal life at point f. Only then are you truly recovered from the stress. For every period of time above the line (in stress territory) you need a balancing time below the line (in relaxation territory). The times spent in each don't necessarily have to be equal, but you do need relaxed time for real recovery.

Stopping is spending time below the line. Stopping can bring true relaxation to some people for the first time in their lives. This is especially true of people who have lived with long-term stressors like chronic illness (of self or others), abusive relationships, unfair work situations, unavoidable meanness, dysfunctional families or businesses, or social conditions so chaotic and uncontrolled that every moment is a moment of crisis wherein anxiety is the norm. It is also true for many people who have slipped into workaholism. Many of us are so used to living above the line, in stress territory, that we can't conceive of why we need to spend time below the line, let alone figure out how to get there.

Because we don't often think of it as stress that we carry personally, I want to call attention to the stress caused by national and international events and personalities, realities that are, for the most part, beyond our control—social stress. Especially in the current era of political polarization, anger, social meanness on all sides, concern for the environment, and the effects of climate change, it is important to acknowledge their significant effect on all of us.

What does time below the line look like for you? These are your clues for Stopovers. It will be different for everyone and even different at various times of your life. Is it walking, swimming, loafing at your ease, watching trees, or being with a poem? The essential characteristic of time below the line is recovery of balance.

Stillpoints are the good friends of relaxation. Breathing and remembering are natural relaxants: they cause the body's autonomic nervous system to relax and recover. To increase the relaxation factor, add a few stretches, notice where you are holding tension in your body, and then breathe relaxing energy into it.

CHAPTER 28
The Gift of Solitude

"Unlike achieving things worth having, to achieve things worth being usually requires long periods of solitude."

—Meyer Friedman and Ray Rosenman, authors

Being comfortable with aloneness is the gift of solitude. It also includes the gift of introspection, which is the ability to look into yourself. Silence is often an attendant benefit. Post-millennial life affords most of us very little solitude, and yet time alone is essential to a balanced life.

"Solitude is a basic human need. We need to get away from the noise and from being with other people," says Anthony Storr, a British psychologist who has written extensively on solitude.

A lot happens when you are alone. Recall the poet Rilke's words: "I am the rest between two notes" that are "reconciled," but only in that "dark interval." What happens in a dark interval is subtle and slow, with gentle nuances. When you try to imagine a dark interval between two notes in a piece of music, it seems to be a place where you must trust. You have to let go of the note that is now finished, which is no longer needed, indeed that is now dead. But the new note is not yet there. This is also a place of solitude in which you wonder: Will the new note really come? Will it be what I expect and need right now?

The dark interval is a place of transformation. At this moment of pause, your song has come just so far. When this momentary pause is finished the song will be new, transformed, and perhaps even sent to a new octave or key. But one thing is sure: it will not be the same. After this pause it will be a new and different song.

"With...devices attached to us all the time; we've lost our stamina for aloneness. You have to bring silence into your life in order to...develop properly. And we've gotten uncomfortable with silence. But we can't have deep conversations with ourselves...when we're distracted."
—Dave Murphy, quoting the *Bainbridge Podcast*, in *SF Chronicle*

So solitude transforms. When you come from a time of aloneness, you are a different you. The transformative nature of solitude underscores the overall significance of Stopping. The success of your life depends to a great extent upon the quality of the pauses between the events of your life. The cumulative effect of the pauses determines not only the greatness of the music but, more importantly, whether *this* is the song *you* want to be singing.

It is not accidental that the great spiritual leaders of history spent a great deal of time withdrawn, apart, or alone; that is, Stopped.

One of the goals of solitude is to be comfortable with your own company, to get to know and like yourself better, and to appreciate the wonderful work of art you are. Are you not used to thinking of yourself that way? If not, please try it. Solitude will help. Often the difference between solitude and loneliness is friendship with yourself.

I don't in any way mean to say that those who are not attracted to solitude have low self-esteem. Natural introversion or extroversion is influential too. People who tend to be introverted are naturally more interested in the internal activity of the soul, while extroverts are more attracted to the soul's expressions in the outside world. One is not better than the other; they are just different. Introverts might seek solitude more easily and more often, but we all need it to some degree.

Anthony Storr also says that "the capacity to be alone... becomes linked with self-discovery and self-realization and with becoming aware of one's deepest needs, feelings, and impulses." When you are alone, many things can happen that busyness and the presence of others disallows: feelings, understandings, remembrances, realizations, priorities, decisions, graces, and so on.

Solitude is the place for introspection: looking into your own soul and discovering there who you are, examining your life, and taking stock. It is the place that allows the internal scanning of Stopping to happen, and thus is perhaps the most fearful of the six traits because it allows things to come up. It is also the trait that, when embraced, can bring you previously unknown peace and calm when you discover that what is there isn't as bad as you had feared.

———

"The mind is sharper and keener
in seclusion and uninterrupted solitude...
Be alone, that is the secret of invention; be alone,
that is when ideas are born."
—Nikola Tesla, inventor

———

Sue Halpern has also written on solitude. Her lesson in *Migrations to Solitude* is that "the days got longer. The texture of our lives became smoother." She gets to the nature of Stopping when she says, "I had set up this paradigm, in which you either live in solitude—you are completely alone—or you live as the rest of us do. I see that it doesn't work that way. I see now that there are degrees of solitude, and it's more about calmness." Her "degrees of solitude" are the Stillpoints, Stopovers, and Grinding Halts of Stopping.

If being alone is daunting to you—as it is for many—try it in small increments and with an easy way out if you need it. Start with a Stillpoint of just a few moments alone, but with others close by, and build up to a Stopover of a couple of hours on an isolated beach or in a park. Each increment will increase your comfort, peace, and calm.

A temptation with solitude is to see only isolation from others rather than solitude with self. Doris Grumbach, in *Fifty Days of Solitude,* says, "What others regard as a retreat from them or a rejection of them is not those things at all but instead a breeding ground for greater friendship, a culture for deeper involvement, eventually, with them." The purpose of solitude is to improve moments of companionship. Stopping is not at all isolationist— just as the purpose of Stopping is going, so the purpose of solitude is that, when you *are* with people, you are more present and responsive.

I am often asked, "Can you do Stopping with someone else?" I would rather say that you can do Stopping at the same time as someone else, and probably in the same place, but the nature of Stopping in all three forms is solitary. Whether it is for one minute or one month, it is a coming back to *yourself*, which is by nature an individual act.

Another common question about Stopping is, "Can watching television be Stopping?" For children and young people, definitely not. For adults? No, not really. It's certainly not for me. For some reason, when the TV is on, I cannot *not* attend to it. But I have a friend who can totally space out in front of the TV. It can be blaring and obnoxious, and he really is capable of not "hearing" it. For people like him, perhaps having the TV on in the same room where you're Stopping can possibly be a low-grade, first-attempt, hardly-better-than-nothing way to Stop.

Writer Sharon Herbstman, discussing the physical and psychological benefits of solitude, says, "Watching television and sleeping don't count; the benefits of solitude come from being able to think freely." I agree.

I don't know how to define noise, but I know it when I hear it. Noise robs us of attention, relaxation, and solitude. Unfortunately, it is all around us, in the country as well as the city. So one of the dearest results of solitude is silence. For starters, "Silence is one of the simplest, most valuable relaxation tools we have," says Edwin Kelley, director of the Insight Meditation Society. On its own, it brings you down below the stress line. Can you identify oases of solitude that are also places of quiet in your part of the world? The cool quiet of an empty church? A museum? The woods near your home? A quiet corner of a nearby park?

"Silence is golden," we were told as children by adults who wanted peace and quiet. Now we know what they meant. Silence also comes in a different but no less appreciated form: the absence of words. English novelist George Eliot said,

"Blessed is the man who, having nothing to say, abstains from giving us wordy evidence of the fact." In my counseling office, I kept a small, framed reminder to myself: "It often shows fine command of the language to say nothing."

Be by yourself. Be quiet. Just be. These are the gifts of solitude and its attendant silence.

CHAPTER 29
The Gift of Boundaries

"Healthy boundaries are flexible enough that we can choose what to let in and what to keep out."

—Anne Katherine, author

Emotional boundaries are a complex psychological subject. The ability to know where you end and the other person begins, to be clear about what is emotionally yours and what is not, and to have people in your life in the places and in the ways that you want them, these are all beneficial for Stopping. Having strong but flexible emotional boundaries means being able to successfully live in a community. This gift encourages your involvement with the world, while helping you avoid unhealthy enmeshment with it.

An easy way to understand boundaries is by thinking of yourself as a house. When the house across the street burns down, you feel bad, but you have not burned down, and you go on about your life. When someone gives the house next to you a new coat of paint, you are perhaps happy for that house, but you don't brag about it, because it is not your coat of paint.

And as for people, (continuing to use a house as a metaphor), there are some you may want outside your gate, some you want in your living room, a few you want in your kitchen, those that you want in the attic, one that you want in your bedroom, and so on. Having good boundaries is having everyone where you want them and not necessarily where they want to be. Now what does this have to do with Stopping?

It's really only with some degree of Stopping, particularly Stopovers and Grinding Halts, that you can find out what your house is like and where everyone is in your house. Stopping is like saying, "Okay, everybody out of here for a while and I'll tell you when—and if—you can come back and where I want you!" Maybe you'll find out there is no one at all in your house or even inside your garden gate, and you would like to have some people there. Only when we notice where our boundaries are (or aren't) can we make choices about them.

Longer forms of Stopping, as well as Stillpoints, also help to distinguish another boundary issue: which are truly your feelings and which are not. Another way of saying this is that Stopping helps you know the difference between yourself and everyone else.

I once observed a family in an urban park having a picnic lunch: mother, father, and two small children. The parents began to argue. As the parents' argument escalated to the point of yelling at each other, I observed the children's emotional states change to mimic their parents'. The children began pouting, clutching at their parents, whimpering, crying, and eventually screaming. As the parents ended/resolved their difference, the children, too, went back to a state of peaceful picnicking. The children could not distinguish their own feelings from their parents'. That's appropriate for children, but unhealthy for adults. Your pain is not mine, nor is mine yours. We can care about each other—have compassion—without losing our boundaries.

The ability to build community is an important result of healthy boundaries. In *Intimacy and Solitude*, Stephanie Dowrick, speaking of intimacy, says, "Without some acceptance of that 'essential aloneness' which is part of the human condition, the experience of closeness [to others] is often difficult." Her "essential aloneness" is what I call being boundaried. There's a paradox again: by clarifying boundaries, by recognizing what distinguishes us from one another, we have the ability to become closer, and thus the community is served. To reiterate: the purpose of the aloneness of Stopping is to be able and competent to form relationships, friendships, and intimacy with other people as those opportunities come to us.

During Stopping, especially the remembering part, self-identity is strengthened and clarified. Remembering where you came from and who you are adds power to your borders so that you don't lose yourself in others and don't allow others to lose themselves in you. When we are together in this way, we can be effective.

Openness

An important part of being a person of clear and strong boundaries involves the quality of openness, an ability to receive the gifts the world has to offer and to learn the lessons of life. It implies boundaries that are flexible—that is, boundaries that are under your control. What I most want to communicate by the word openness is contained in the following words from the poet Rainer Maria Rilke, addressed to a young colleague: "If the angel deigns to come it will be because you have convinced her, not by tears but by your humble resolve to be always beginning: to be a beginner."

To be a beginner is a goal of all spiritual endeavors. The beginner knows she has something to learn; the expert "knows" the answers and he is thus cut off from possibilities.

When you see yourself as a beginner, you become receptive, open. Being receptive is the ability to take something or someone into your heart and mind when you want to, when it serves you or others, when it's true and just, and the ability to keep it out when it fails your conditions.

Why is receptivity necessary? Consider it as the most important way of gaining information, insight, knowledge, or anything. To get anything, you must be receptive to it. If we are not comfortable with being receptive, we'll miss much of what comes our way; we just don't see it, even though it may have appeared before our eyes.

Think of it this way: If all you are is action, you never get the feedback you desperately need to understand the result of your action. It is the heart of learning to know what happened as a result of what you did. Then, when you return to your active mode, you will be acting in a way that is based on the information you got by being receptive. You have created a feedback loop of information and power.

"Open" is a good way to describe the person who is capable of receiving what is available to them: spontaneous expressions of life, surprises, and new things, blatant as well as subtle epiphanies, which are all those big or little moments when we realize something, get something for the first time, have a "vision," see something manifested like never before, or achieve a new understanding of how life is and how we fit into it.

"I have always loved a window, especially an open one."
—Wendell Berry, poet

Effective listening is also the result of developing healthy openness and flexible boundaries. Instead of thinking of what you are going to say in response as someone speaks to you, you listen—you become receptive—to the other person. You take in consciously what they say, which means you notice their tone of voice, their body language, their vocabulary, and, thus, the real meaning of what they are saying. In this way, your response is much more likely to be appropriate, accurate, and effective.

Openness involves being open to ideas and movements that might be outside your comfort zone, not in your usual, inherited way of thinking, or that are controversial. Ideas, for example, about ecology, climate change, racism, political ideologies, social customs, and even family traditions: these indeed can be difficult to be open to, especially when your whole life and way of being feels challenged. This of course applies to both poles of progressive and conservative ideologies and to all in between.

Openness emphasizes listening (not talking), receiving (not giving), being cared for (not taking care of), being quiet (not noisy), observing (not acting), noticing (not commenting), and learning (not teaching). Please note that the characteristics in parentheses are not, obviously, in any way bad or negative; they're just not what is needed for the gift of Stopping that we're talking about here: having healthy boundaries and, specifically, being open.

CHAPTER 30
The Gift of Embracing Your Shadow

"Keep your face to the sunshine and you cannot see the shadow."

—Helen Keller, author

Shadow (as a specific term) comes to us from the psychologist Carl Jung. He called it an archetype, or a pattern of perception, that we all hold in our consciousness. It refers to that secret and often negative and fearful part of ourselves that we generally like to keep hidden or pretend doesn't exist. Jung's insight was to identify the shadow as a positive force and a means to self-understanding. A hidden shadow can cause problems; it's an enemy we don't know. But if we look at that hidden part of ourselves and learn to embrace it, we grow in self-understanding and transform an enemy into a wonderful gift.

The process of Stopping allows time to encounter and ultimately embrace the shadow. When Stopped, I see things in myself that I normally ignore. The self-conversation in my head might go like this: Yes, I see that my shadow is sometimes a jealous tyrant; I don't like that part of myself but I have to admit, in truth, that it's there; generally my feelings of jealousy are under control but sometimes they jump out and get me into trouble and I do and say what I would rather, given my rational preference, not do or say. If I acknowledge that jealous self, try to find out what he craves, wants, and needs to tell me, maybe I have a good chance to turn that energy to good use.

Embracing the shadow is acknowledging that nothing is either black or white, but everything is a portion of both. When we project our shadow out—that is, when I point to you as the one who is causing all the trouble—we deny it in ourselves. The truth is there is no "evil empire," no groups or individuals that are the cause of our suffering and the world's evil. *We all are the causes.* When we deny or avoid our shadow, it not only has its nasty way with us, it can cause great harm, even death, to others.

Many of our world's serious crises and conflicts are clearly caused by leaders who have no acquaintance at all with their shadow; they simply project all that they see as wrong or evil onto others.

Facing our shadow during Stopping can be scary. "When one first sees the shadow clearly," says Jungian scholar John A. Sanford, "one is more or less aghast." When I was a boy, my brother and I would listen to *The Shadow* on the radio. The part of the program that I remember vividly is the beginning with the scary music and a man's deep, sinister voice asking, "What evil lurks in the hearts of men? The Shadow knows!" The voice would trail off in menacing and foreboding laughter. It scared us. One's own shadow can still scare us. What indeed *does* my shadow know? Do I also know it? Will it surprise me and get me and others into trouble? What if I can't handle it? That's where courage comes in.

Aleksandr Solzhenitsyn, Russian dissident and novelist, said, "If only there were evil people somewhere insidiously committing evil deeds, and it were necessary only to separate them from the rest of us and destroy them. But the line dividing good and evil cuts through the heart of every human being." That includes mine and yours. If we could have the courage to embrace our scary shadows, we would thereby take a giant leap to heal the world's deep and lasting pain.

Stopping is a process whereby you can—especially if this is scary for you—gradually shake hands with your shadow. By first specifically acknowledging only your *desire* at some time to embrace your shadow, you can bring some safety and control to the process by taking it at your own pace.

"If you bring forth what is within you, what you bring forth will save you. If you do not bring forth what is in you, what you do not bring forth will destroy you."
—attributed to Jesus of Nazareth in the Gospel of Thomas

Scott Peck, psychiatrist and bestselling author, in dealing with the shadow speaks of the central defect of evil as being not the sin itself but the refusal to acknowledge it. The refusal to acknowledge our dark tendencies is the central defect, not the dark tendencies themselves; they are part of our humanity. As Solzhenitsyn said, those tendencies are always with us. Both good and evil are in *all* our hearts. Only when I can acknowledge *all* parts of me can I move from childhood to maturity, from isolation to community, and from running and covering to peace and equanimity.

The shadow is also a trickster. It can make a lie look like the truth, a fiction like a fact, and a doubt like a conviction.

Because it's a trickster, it can take many forms, even the form of innocence.

The gift of acknowledging your shadow is the antidote to the often-dangerous oversimplification of the innocent Pollyanna. During the period of training for my counseling degree, I had the opportunity to take a short class from Daniel Berrigan, SJ, the renowned Jesuit peace activist, author, and teacher. He spoke to us eloquently about "terrible innocence." Terrible innocence is an attitude which, while looking into the face of evil, prompts us to deny it, avoid it, to pretend not to notice it, or to feign ignorance while, in our hearts, we really know what's going on. It brings the false innocence of sweetness and light to a moment of possibly serious harm. That indeed is terrible innocence; terrible because it allows me to stand idle in the presence of evil. That's also a well-hidden shadow.

That's what Stopping can help us to uncover and heal.

CHAPTER 31
The Gift of Purpose

"A calling may be postponed, avoided, intermittently missed...but eventually it will out."

—James Hillman, psychologist

Purpose is the wonderful gift of Stopping that encourages us to go out from ourselves, to listen to what we might hear from the universe, and to discover our unique role in life. Purpose means that someone or something outside of you is looking at you and calling your name; you are being called to accomplish an objective, to be someone that only you can be, and to realize what is most essentially you. Another word to express the same idea is *calling*. The idea of *vocation* also serves well. Stopping helps you to clarify or even discover your purpose, to hear your calling, and to realize your vocation.

Purpose is knowing that there is something beyond us. And knowing that there are events, moments, and realities of life that are not immediately identifiable and explainable only by the facts that we can see and prove. The sense of having a purpose gives balance to our human situation: not only do we meet the divine, however you define that, as we look within ourselves, as surely we do, but in the same moments of Stopping, we meet the divine in the call that reaches to us from beyond ourselves. This beyondness is the distinctive characteristic that underscores the importance of this gift of Stopping.

Having purpose acknowledges that you are named to be something that only you can be. Your challenge is to find it, discover it, wrestle with it, or do whatever is necessary to realize it.

James Hillman, an always insightful, if controversial, author, writes about this idea from a somewhat different perspective in his book *The Soul's Code*. His theory, the acorn theory, briefly stated, is that we are all born with a calling and the object of life is to discover and realize that calling. Hillman calls this *growing down* into the acorn. Instead of looking ahead to what we might become as we try to realize our inner potential, he suggests that we also look back at the call we have been given at birth, even before birth, and try to allow its fulfillment. Realizing one's calling is to look out to the world for signs as well as back to the seed or gift with which we were born.

I believe he's on to something. If we miss this element of our Stopping experiences, or if we only concentrate on validating very narrow desires and yearnings, we run a real risk of seeing the world purely subjectively and from a limited point of view, and thus run the risk of becoming selfish, overbearing, patronizing, and self-righteous. It can also make it easy to get stuck blaming someone else for our problems and to take ourselves way too seriously.

Trying to identify, to clarify, and to respond to our purpose, or trying to hear and realize our call, takes our gaze out to the world's horizons to see what in the world or what in the heavens is calling on us for service, for help, for joy, for entertainment, or for whatever it is that only we can give. And it also takes our gaze back into our personal histories to search for clues. It frees us from allowing introspection to become overly impressed with subjective intuitions and gives the objective intuitions a chance.

"What you seek is seeking you."
—Rumi, poet

Purpose and calling have a power of their own; they always want to come out and have life. Having a sense of your calling is having a sense of the presence of something other than yourself. Perhaps when you were younger there was a moment when you came in touch with that something beyond. You knew that you wanted to do something and to be something. Perhaps it just struck you and you knew, or maybe it was more subtle. As Hillman says, "The call may have been more like gentle pushings in the stream in which you drifted unknowingly to a particular spot on the bank." As you look back, you have a sense that something beyond you was involved. It is also important to remember that it is never too late to hear your call; now is *always* the right time.

Hillman tells a story about world famous singer Ella Fitzgerald. As a young girl she was in an amateur night event. She was introduced: "Miss Fitzgerald is going dance for us... Hold it, hold it. Now what's your problem, honey?...Correction, folks. Miss Fitzgerald has changed her mind. She's not going to dance; she's going to sing." She won first prize. Though she had meant to dance, something told her to sing, and that was the start of a long, successful career. Hillman tells the story to demonstrate his acorn theory and that it sometimes shows itself early and unexpectedly.

The gift of purpose is especially realized during the longer times of Stopovers and Grinding Halts, dealing, as they do, with the broad questions of calling and vocation.

It isn't only the famous people of the world who have a purpose. We all do. And most often it does not make itself known as dramatically or as early as Ella Fitzgerald's. Purpose is not always a specific talent or service, but more commonly an underlying principle or principles which guide one's life. Stopping is very much about recognizing those principles, realizing your calling, and identifying and fulfilling your purpose. We have to be still, quiet, undistracted, and awake enough to hear it. For to miss it would be tragic.

PART IV
Challenges and Discoveries

CHAPTER 32
Moving Down to the Roots

"There is more to life than increasing its speed."

—Mohandas Gandhi, philosopher

This last section focuses on the challenges you are likely to meet as you incorporate Stopping into your life, as well as the various ways you will discover your own style and personal way to do it—creating your own art of Stopping.

We are at a critical point on our journey with Stopping because we now have enough information to see that Stopping asks us to do something radical. Stopping is not complicated, is not difficult to understand, and is not even difficult to do. But it is radical. Stopping is not slowing down. Stopping is stopping. The effect will be to slow us down, yes, but the primary act is doing nothing, ceasing activity, and being still.

"Radical?" you might think, "I don't do radical!" But radical can be very simple. Banish the common images associated with it—starvation fasts, street riots, or someone's liberation army—and simply move the energy down deep and into your roots.

That's what radical really means. Here's Webster's definition of radical: "From a root or relating to the origin: fundamental." Stopping brings you to your origins and to what is fundamentally you. It brings you to your true home. It reaches deeply into your soul. And it's common not to go there often; we're not used to the territory because the problem of too much is keeping us distracted.

Take a moment and allow yourself to form a mental image of a tree. What you probably have in your mind's eye is only part of a tree: the part you see. But the whole tree includes a root structure as broad and deep as the branches are high and wide. A whole tree is a trunk between two equal masses of branches and roots.

Stopping is an energy that is radical because it takes you down to the roots of the tree that is you, down to the sources of your life. Those roots, which are not so obvious, but which are essential, are the necessary balance to the more active, external, and obvious branches of life.

So if Stopping is so great and wonderful, is so easy to do, and gives so many benefits, why don't we all just do it? Because we have received powerful anti-Stopping messages from society telling us it is wasting time, and because many of us are afraid of what we'll discover down there in the roots of ourselves. We're unfamiliar with the territory and we often want to avoid it, if possible.

The goal of this section is to help you feel competent and confident as you deal with the challenges you may encounter with Stopping. To that end, please keep these important facts in mind: the fears you might face as you are Stopped are almost never as bad as you might think; there are ways to deal with them that are satisfying and effective; if you have some overwhelming fears, there are safe ways to get help; and not to face your fears is to leave unexplored way too much of a vibrant, gift-filled life.

Our first challenge is the intense and potent anti-Stopping messages our culture has been imparting to us since childhood.

CHAPTER 33
When Society Says "Don't"

"We have lived not in proportion to the number of years we have spent on the earth, but in proportion as we have enjoyed."

—Henry David Thoreau, essayist

We live in a world that is not very open or friendly to Stopping. Our society's voices often say, "Keep going, don't stop!" In order to Stop, we need to release the hold that our culture's unspoken but powerful messages have on us. Here are some of the ideas behind the anti-Stopping voices:

- Leisure is a luxury you really can't afford.
- Resting is a waste of time.
- Pleasure-seekers are selfish.
- Success means working more hours.
- You have to keep up with the neighbors.
- Doing nothing is slothful and lazy.
- If it's faster, it's better.
- Growth is always good.
- Money is the bottom line.

- More is always better than less.
- Play is only for children.

The list of lies is endless, and it is often difficult to resist believing them. They can sound convincing. We often hear them coming from our own lips.

When we stop to think about them, we know that these statements are not true. But *only* when we stop to think about them. If we don't, the danger is that they will have their way with us. We get distracted, we forget, and it's easier to just go along with them. Notice that they all argue against Stopping and taking time out for yourself and for those around you.

There are also many voices saying that life is a most serious business. But just what does *serious* mean? The dictionary indicates that its first and most important meaning is "thoughtful." So in that case, yes, life must be serious, and we must live it thoughtfully. But not grimly. The word *serious*, with its meanings of "grim, heavy, no-fun-allowed, and painful," I would suggest, is not applicable to Stopping.

"Rest is not idleness, and sometimes to lie on the grass under the trees on a summer's day, listening to the murmur of the water, or watching the clouds float across the blue sky, is by no means a waste of time."
—John Lubbock, scientist

Often, it seems, organized religions can give the idea that life is serious in the grim kind of way. One need only think of the imperiousness of Vatican pronouncements, of the seven deadly sins, and of the rules, regulations, and prohibitions of many religions. The international memorial to the Protestant Reformation in Geneva, Switzerland, visually supports this as well. The memorial is a three-hundred-foot-long wall of granite with fifteen-foot statues of an unsmiling Calvin, Knox, and Cromwell who are protected by an equally long moat of water; it says serious with a capital S. And the depictions of Moses with the Ten Commandments? Nothing to be taken lightly for sure.

I want to be the first to support religions in their effort to make us more thoughtful about how we live our lives. I also want to be the first to speak against their unfortunate propensity to kill people's spirits with oppressive, grim, and meaningless injunctions and attitudes. Life is hard enough on its own. Let's not needlessly multiply sins. We have enough of those, too.

Robert Ornstein and David Sobel understand this idea and express it in their book *Healthy Pleasures.* They say, "Combining an archaic religiosity with a sensory-deprived world is to place two prisons together. The result is a life lost not only to this world but to the next." "Archaic religiosity" is a false or excessive religiousness. Combine that with our tendency to ignore the pleasures of the natural world and, say the authors, you are succeeding not only in missing life on earth but are also trying to bully your way into a very restrictive heaven with a frowning and determined grimace on your face. Who would want to go to that kind of heaven?

Stopping is time spent with ourselves, especially the longer times of Stopovers and Grinding Halts, that we all need in order to keep our perspective and not take ourselves too seriously.

Writer Mark Matousek tells of a wonderful moment in his life that demonstrates this idea. For half an hour he was trying to explain his spirituality to his friend, expounding on all the intricacies of self and no-self, on liberation and enlightenment, and on the teachings of inspiring gurus and saints. When he was finished, his friend, after a long pause, smiled and asked, "Do you mean being kind?"

Stopping says, "No!" to the voices that say, "It's selfish to take time for yourself," "Life is by its very nature a grimly serious affair," and "Laugh at others' foibles but not at your own." In this way, Stopping is countercultural. It is not afraid to say no and say it strongly. It encourages you to discover your own voice, your own priorities, your own wisdom, and your own fun.

"At the center of your being you have the answer; you know who you are, and you know what you want."

—Anonymous

The problems we have with Stopping are generally not intellectual problems. Often we know exactly what is good for us and what, given our best moment, we would choose. Our problem is the one St. Paul groused about in his letter to the community in Rome: "Those things I wish to do, I do not; those I wish to avoid, those I do" (Rom. 7:17–19). Stopping is a way to assure that the things you want are the things you actually do.

Speaking of St. Paul, here's another opportunity to remember to be patient with yourself as you go about incorporating Stopping into your life. Paul was so hurried, driven, and work oriented that he had to be Stopped. He was literally knocked off his horse to the ground and made blind so that he had to spend

Stopover time in Damascus doing nothing in order to become more fully awake and remember who he was. Sound familiar? When he did awaken and remember, his vision returned and he changed the world.

CHAPTER 34
"I'm Afraid!"

"I've lived! I've got to find out what to do now!"

—Agnes Gooch, in Auntie Mame

"I am afraid of the whole world," said poet Pablo Neruda. Fear is endemic in our society. So as we move our energy and our focus down to our roots, the first feeling we are likely to experience is fear.

I wonder if you know that wonderful scene from the movie *Auntie Mame* in which the comical and trouble-prone Agnes Gooch, played by Peggy Cass, painfully pregnant and bewildered, bumbles up the stairs in search of Auntie Mame and says in all her innocent confusion, "Well I've lived! I've got to find out what to do now!?" Her question rises out of the place of fear that we all carry with us at our roots.

If there is any idea that is common to all systems of wisdom, religion, and philosophy, it is the truth that the greatest challenge of one's life is oneself. Fear? Of course. Again the poet sees what we all need to see. In this case, let's look at what Pablo Neruda sees. Read the following poem aloud, if your situation allows; reading it aloud will tend to slow it down and bring it home to you.

Fear

Everyone is after me to exercise,
get in shape, play football,
rush about, even go swimming and flying.
Fair enough.

Everyone is after me to take it easy.
They all make doctor's appointments for me,
eyeing me in that quizzical way.
What is it?

Everyone is after me to take a trip,
to come in, to leave, not to travel,
to die and, alternatively, not to die.
It doesn't matter.

Everyone is spotting oddnesses
in my innards, suddenly shocked
by radio-awful diagrams.
I don't agree with them.

Everyone is picking at my poetry
with their relentless knives and forks,
trying, no doubt, to find a fly.
I am afraid.

I am afraid of the whole world,
afraid of cold water, afraid of death.
I am as all mortals are,
unable to be patient.

And so, in these brief, passing days,
I shall put them out of my mind.
I shall open up and imprison myself

with my most treacherous enemy,
Pablo Neruda.

What does Neruda tell us about fear? Here's how the poem gets into my head: Everyone is trying to give me advice. Do this, do that! Don't do this, don't do that! I know I'm sick, but I'm still here and I'm still in charge! So I will ignore all of you and do what is most important at a time like this, face my fears and face what has always been my most serious challenge—me.

Between the lines (Remember the spaces between the notes? It's where the most interesting things happen), I picture Neruda with his wise old face, leaning close to us and whispering into our ears: "I am writing this for you, the one who's reading it. Do it now. Spend time with yourself now, while you still can."

This part of the book takes Neruda's words to heart and Agnes Gooch's question seriously. We will lock ourselves up with our most double-crossing enemies, us, and we will answer Agnes's question, "Now what!?" Let's form the question like this: "Now that I am Stopped, even for a moment, how do I assure myself that I will be okay and that I will not have to face more than I can deal with?"

Stopping will feel safe when fears no longer have their way with you. The fears will not necessarily be gone but they will not be in control. And, paradoxically, it is by moving into your fears that you will move out of them.

That paradox is the goal here, to move out of our fears by first moving into them. Moving into them involves three simple processes: noticing, naming, and narrating. Your fears will gradually diminish and lose their power over you as you learn these three processes. First notice, or note, your fears and take them into account; then name your fears; and then narrate, or tell your story of these fears to someone else, to the world.

Recall the story of Naaman. He was the general who was hesitant to cure his illness by following the prophet's advice to wash seven times in the river because it seemed too simple and silly to him. Now is a good time to recall the lesson of the story: to respect the power of simple acts.

Please don't underestimate the power of these simple acts of the soul: noticing, naming, and narrating. Keep in mind the reason for exploring our way of dealing with our feelings of fear: The inability to be still and quiet and at peace—necessary for Stopping—is most often caused by unidentified and unexpressed feelings of fear.

CHAPTER 35
Notice, Name, and Narrate

"Silent, hidden enemies are more to be feared than those that are openly expressed."

—Cicero, philosopher and statesman

The *first* and vitally important step in dealing with your feelings of fear is to notice them, take note of them, acknowledge that they exist and are present. Without this step, the whole process is doomed.

Noticing means that you do not place a value judgment on yourself for whatever you are noticing. Whatever comes up, the first thing to do is just let it come up and let it be. That's noticing.

I am often tempted to allow judgment to jump right in and ruin it all. The judgment of *I shouldn't be having this feeling of fear* is as appropriate as thinking *I shouldn't have brown eyes.* The fear is just there, that's all. And it's morally neutral; no guilt and no virtue are involved. For those who have been raised in highly structured religious systems, not judging ourselves for feelings that come on their own can be a challenge.

Internal Chatter

Often the first thing that gets your attention as you are trying to notice what you are feeling is that, even though your body might be Stopped and at rest, your mind goes racing on. And does it race! Sometimes it seems that my mind has a mind of its own. The internal chatter seems endless.

These are the "tapes" that play over and over in your head and create noise in your mind. Your noisy self-talk can just keep on going, whether you are aware of it or not, whether you are listening or not, and even whether you seem to care or not.

By calling attention to your internal chatter you will gain a bit of control over it and maybe even quiet it down occasionally. Quieting the noise of internal chatter is a goal of Stopping and—understanding this was a breakthrough for me—this is a goal no one can ever fully accomplish. It is a challenging task, a part of what Jack Kornfield in A Path with Heart calls "stopping the war" we carry within us. Saints, monks, and spiritual masters all tell us that they are still working on it, so we must be easy on ourselves. It's simply part of our human nature.

What the masters also tell us is just let it come and then let it go. Any enemy—in this case the annoying chatter—that has been spotted is in a much weaker position than when it had the power of being hidden or unnoticed.

So just notice your feelings of fear. That's all. Noticing is the opposite of repression or pushing away fears. Instead, it is turning and acknowledging them: *Oh, yes, I am afraid of people who talk loudly, I am afraid of heights, of dogs, of dark and isolated places…or of what might come up if I become quiet enough to really notice what's there.*

I want to say this about hidden fears: don't be surprised if there are none. In my experience with people in therapy, that happens a lot. The fears they expected to find when they turned and faced themselves simply were not there. They can truthfully say, along with Thoreau, "Nothing is so much to be feared as fear." Eighty years later, FDR would say the same thing in his first inaugural address: "We have nothing to fear but fear itself."

But let's say that you indeed find some fears. What would noticing them look like? If you were to eavesdrop on my mind as I considered my fears before leaving the ministry, you would have heard something like this:

I am afraid of losing the values that have supported my entire life up to this point. Am I losing my faith? I fear breaking my public vows. What will my family and colleagues think of me? I fear being called a failure. I am afraid that I will not be able to support myself since this is all I am trained to do.

Believe me the list could go on. I could have said, as Neruda said, "I am afraid. I am afraid of the whole world."

During my month-long Grinding Halt, I was able to notice my fears. I just let them come and noted their presence. I logged them, saying, "There's one," "there's another," and "Here's another one too." They just came on their own because I was not covering them. I knew they were there, and they "knew" I knew.

Noticing is like being open: you simply take in the information and mark the presence of, be aware of, note, and store the data. I believe you will find that noticing will be more powerful for you than you expected.

Step two is to name your fears. By naming, I mean any process by which you talk to or talk about your hidden fears. Naming can include actually giving the fear a name ("Your name is Fear of Failure!"). Naming often involves personifying the feelings as if they were persons in order to interact with them. That automatically happens when you talk to them: "Hello, Fear of Disapproval, here you are again"; "Oh, here's Fear of Being a Bad Leader, she's an old friend"; "Oh no, it's you, Fear of the Worst Thing Happening, I thought you were gone for good!"

Naming is important because it gives you power over the thing named. Just as when you name a pet or—especially—your own child, you thus assume a position of power and responsibility over it, so with naming fears.

By naming you also are accepting ownership. In effect, you are saying, "These are *my* fears. I acknowledge and accept that they are mine and no one else's." Think about it: if they belong to you, as indeed they do, then you have power over them.

Fears named and addressed are fears weakened. Now, you have *them*; they don't have *you*.

An effective way to use naming during your Stopping, even during the briefer times, is to name the fears that you hold in your body. Often the body remembers what the mind forgets; it can hold on to fears and make them present to you through pain, tension, aches, stiffness, and soreness. So when you experience an unusual discomfort in your stomach, you might ask, "I wonder what was wrong with that tuna sandwich I had for lunch?" More accurate questions would be, "Who did I have lunch with?" or "What were we talking about?" When your neck and shoulder tension become severe, maybe it's not just the lack of exercise but the fear you are carrying there. Thus identified, the fear is weakened. By naming, you are asking the right questions.

There is one fear that must be named here; it's the fear that is almost always a part of every other fear, especially those that might come to us while we are Stopped. Its name is Fear of Death. Even more powerfully and importantly its name is Fear of My Death.

Here I want only to give it a name: "You are Fear of My Own Death." In naming it I hope to encourage you to acknowledge its presence and to become, if you are not already, comfortable and familiar with it. That we are all in the process of dying need not be sad or depressing. Indeed, embracing that reality can become wonderfully liberating. Our principle still—maybe especially—holds true here: by moving into our fears we move out of them.

The third and final step in dealing with your feelings of fear is to narrate them. In other words, tell them in some way to the world—express them externally—get them out of you and into the world in some identifiable way. The telling brings relief. And the more secret and hidden the fear, the more effective and relieving the telling.

"I wonder how all those who do not write, compose, or paint can manage to escape the...fear which is inherent in a human situation."
—Graham Greene, novelist

To whom can you tell your fears? This is often not an easy question. The answers can be different for everyone. Is it a spouse or partner? Often they are the most difficult to confide in, either because they are involved in the fear and feel it too closely also or they are too threatened to be able to understand. A parent or sibling? A fortunate number of us have developed such a relationship with a member of the immediate family. Often, though, it will be a friend. A friend with whom you can talk about who you really are. What a gift! A gift to treasure if you have it; one to cultivate if you don't.

Before you share your fear with another, it is like you are alone in your home and hear someone rattling the front door. Your friend's reassurance is a familiar voice outside the door: "Don't be afraid. It's just me." What a comforting announcement. Fear is immediately transformed into connection. You are no longer alone with your fears.

Fear can never completely leave us. In a way, it's necessary. We would not be safe without it. Fear helps us to be careful. You would not want to lose completely, for example, a fear of height, of dangerous substances, of aggressive people, or of snarling animals. To do so would be to endanger yourself. No, the fears we are speaking of here are the irrational, the unsubstantiated, the inhibiting, and the self-damaging.

Fear can be told in many ways, not just to another individual, but to the world. Throughout human history, fears have been the motivation of great artistic and scientific expression. As novelist Graham Greene reminds us in the epigraph quoted above, fear motivates artists to speak to the world about their most profound insights. Is this a way for you to narrate your fear? What can your fear lead you to express artistically to all of us who would welcome your perceptions?

The next chapter tells three stories of ways to accomplish the three steps in dealing with these and all feelings.

CHAPTER 36
Expressing Feelings: Three Stories

"The most terrifying thing is to accept
oneself completely."

—Carl Jung, psychologist

Stoned

Some of the most wonderful years of my ministry were spent on my three-and-a-half-year assignment to work in Cali, Colombia, South America. Some companions and I had a scary experience there. We got stoned.

No, it's not what you might be thinking. This was well before the time of the Cali cartel. By stoned, I mean literally. Four of us, the staff of our parish, were driving to the airport to meet a new member of our team. There had been a recent boycott of all the public buses due to a drastic increase in bus fares. The people simply stopped using the buses, the buses quit running, and the city was paralyzed. Outbreaks of violence were reported; often private cars were attacked. But all that was over; it was safe to go out now—or so we thought.

We were in the riot before we knew it. And that we got out of it unharmed still amazes me. We had to drive through mobs of people with stones, many of them rock sized, as if through a tunnel of terror. The car was hit more than a hundred times—we later counted the dents—the windows were all smashed, and we were totally shaken.

When it was over, we began to tell each other and anyone who would listen about our experience. We still remind each other of it when we meet to this day. It has, for all of us, been in the telling that we have recovered, that we have learned from it, and that we have tried to place the experience within the context of our lives. Imagine trying to keep quiet about such an experience! Even at this moment as I write about it, and thus tell it again, I find new meanings and new lessons, and I remember many more. In the telling the fears are lessened.

The Purse

For me, one of the most powerful moments in the contemporary literature of psychotherapy is a chapter from Irving Yalom's book *Love's Executioner.*

He tells of a client, an older woman, who had been deeply hurt and who needed to learn to trust again. Eventually, during one of their counseling sessions, she simply emptied the contents of her purse and told him stories—meanings, values, feelings—about all the items she carried there and was now showing him, one by one. It was utterly simple and utterly profound, and she left the session more able to trust, less burdened, less fearful. And he, the therapist, said, "I think it was the best hour of therapy I ever gave." By naming her intimate and personal items and narrating her feelings about them, she came significantly closer to being able to trust.

Unthinkable Thought

In the autobiographical *Memories, Dreams, Reflections,* Carl Jung, one of the most eminent physicians and psychologists of the twentieth century, tells a story from when he was about twelve years old. It's a story about overcoming fear by moving into it and noticing, naming, and narrating:

> One fine summer day...I came out of school at noon and went to the cathedral square. The sky was gloriously blue, the day one of radiant sunshine. The roof of the cathedral glittered, the sun sparkling from the new, brightly glazed tiles.
>
> I was overwhelmed by the beauty of the sight, and thought: "The world is beautiful and the church is beautiful, and God made all this and sits above it far away in the blue sky on a golden throne and..." here came a great hole in my thoughts, and a choking sensation. I felt numbed and knew only: "Don't go on thinking now! Something terrible is coming, something I do not want to think, something I dare not even approach...because it would be committing the most frightful of sins."

Jung, the pious son of a clergyman, then describes how he did all he could do to keep the vision away and not give into it, how his mother worried about his odd behavior, how he lost sleep, and how he was deeply fearful that if he let the thought come he would plunge himself directly into hell. This was truly a terrified boy.

After going though much mental anxiety, utterly alone in his painful anguish, he finally was able to resolve his conflict:

> God also desires me to show courage. And if that is so… he will give me his grace… I gathered all my courage, as though I were about to leap forthwith into hellfire, and let the thought come.

> I saw before me the cathedral, the blue sky. God sits on His golden throne, high above the world—and from under the throne an enormous turd falls upon the sparkling new roof, shatters it, and breaks the walls of the cathedral asunder. So that was it! I felt an enormous and indescribable relief.

Clearly, there is much that could be said about the meaning of this earthy and dramatic image. But what is significant for us is that he overcame his fear by moving into it and by letting it come. He says, "Why did God befoul His cathedral? That, for me, was a terrible thought." But it was also an important thought for him, a key element in developing his teaching on the shadow archetype that is pivotal to the way many understand human nature.

This story from Jung demonstrates so clearly the three steps of dealing with feelings of fear, which, in turn may keep you from achieving the stillness that is an essential part of Stopping. The noticing: "Something terrible is coming… Something I do not want to think." The naming: "So that was it!"

The narrating takes a little different twist and reminds us that we are not alone in the challenge of telling our fears to others. Says Jung of his experience at the time it occurred: "It would never have occurred to me to speak of my experience openly… I could never have talked about [it] with friends." He indicates that he finally talked about his experience with his wife, but that was years later. The final narration, of course, was to include it in his memoir. It took him a while, but finally he narrated it.

CHAPTER 37
Some Help in Getting Help

We've Had a Hundred Years of Psychotherapy and the World's Getting Worse

—Title of a book
by James Hillman and Michael Ventura, psychologists

Sometimes noticing, naming, and narrating are not enough, and you need help. If you feel you want to get help as you encounter your fears and challenges, here are a few ideas about counseling to keep in mind.

First, counseling does not have to go on for a long time. Often, what is now called "brief therapy" (in the range of three to fifteen weeks, once a week) is all that it takes. As much as anything, therapy speeds up the healing, the growth, or the problem-solving processes.

Second, you can get competent help at a reasonable price. You might have to look a little harder, but it is possible. Check out mental health clinics and (nonproselytizing) church-sponsored counseling agencies. Trained pastoral counselors are one of the world's most valuable and best-kept secrets.

Third, maybe more appropriate for you would be a mentor, coach, or spiritual director. A mentor is, generally, an older person who is wise, caring, experienced in what you need to learn, willing to help, and someone you can trust. Normally it is not a paid relationship. A coach, picking up its model from the sports world, is someone who is not a professional therapist but is someone who cares, has experience and exposure to basic mental health practice, and to whom you can report regularly for encouragement, advice, or direction. It is most often a paid relationship. A spiritual director is a friendly guide and companion who helps you focus specifically on your spiritual life. This is often a paid relationship, but also sometimes considered part of the service of clergy or religious personnel.

Fourth, most therapy is not only for deeply troubled people but for you and me at moments of challenge and opportunity. Most counseling clients just need a little help over the rough spots. So please don't feel embarrassed or ashamed. In the vast majority of cases, therapy is not about a therapist giving advice to an emotionally ill person; it's about any person looking for a safe place and a skilled, wise companion for a particularly challenging part of his or her journey.

Fifth, shop around. If you feel uncomfortable with the therapist you have for any reason, first talk to them about your feelings and, if it's not possible to resolve them, seek another that you like. The counselor works for you, not the other way around. But, as Hillman and Ventura's intentionally provocative book title at the opening of the chapter implies, all therapy is not equal. Generally, look for counselors who are members of their professional association and are open to take their starting point from what you report is going on with you, not those who try to squeeze you into a system they happen to practice.

And finally, here's a response to the frequent question, "How do I know when it's time to get into therapy?" Echoing Dr. M. Scott Peck's words, "It's time to get into therapy when you feel you can no longer keep moving ahead by yourself as you deal with your fears; when you're really stuck."

I recall, with some chagrin, going into therapy for the first time. I was studying to be a therapist and it was obligatory in my program to be in therapy. Otherwise, I most likely would not have done it at that time. It took me three months to find a therapist. I know of a professor of psychotherapy who had never been in therapy until a crisis during his retirement (he was sixty-eight) forced him to seek solutions. Talk about resistance!

The therapist I found was a gift. Young, bright, earnest, and Jewish. I wondered at first if this would work: Jewish therapist and former Christian minister client. Would he understand my issues? He was skillful. When he did not understand one or another aspect of my world, he would get me to tell him about it. Thus, I was always telling him my stories, which is the best kind of therapy.

CHAPTER 38
"Yes, But..."

"I'm afraid if I stop, I'll never be able to start again!"

—An overworked nurse

Let me anticipate some possible objections to Stopping that might be running through your mind at this point.

Objection: "Look, I already know what will come up for me when I Stop. It's always the same thing, the same old pain (or anger or upset or fear). Why would I want to think of that? It's over and done and there's nothing to be gained but more pain."

Response: The paradox is that the more you move into the same old thing, the less power it will have to cause you pain. The reason it keeps coming up is because it has never been faced, or never faced completely. When you keep the door bolted against the big bad wolf, he stays right outside your door, growling, snarling, and constantly reminding you that he's there. Could you be getting used to having him right outside the door? Is it possible in some way you like him there?

As a student, I had a wonderful spiritual director who was both wise and funny. When I would confess to him, in the pious language of the day, that "I had entertained impure thoughts," he answered, "Heh, heh! Let's get it straight here, kiddo, you didn't entertain them, they entertained you!" So maybe you are used to keeping things out of reach just enough so that they, in some way, "entertain you." Open the door, invite the big bad wolf in, give him a name, get it over with, and move on.

There's another idea to keep in mind as a response to this objection: creative denial. Sometimes denial is not bad; it can even be beneficial. Healthy denial differs from unhealthy denial because it isn't *really* denial, it's temporary avoidance. You see this clearly in some terminally ill people. "This afternoon I don't have cancer. I don't want anybody to mention it at all," said the twelve-year-old girl to her family on the way from the hospital to an afternoon at the zoo. This is an example of creative denial that was used as a respite from the intensity of a painful reality, and it is healthy. So a healthy-denial Stopover might not look like a Stopover at all, but it is.

Objection: "I've tried various things like meditation before and, frankly, I get immensely bored. It isn't that I fear anything, it's just that doing nothing bores me so much that I always move on to something that keeps my interest or that is useful."

Response: Start with Stillpoints. They are so short it is impossible to get bored. But, at a deeper level, please don't be fooled by boredom. It's often a cover for something else. Begin, like with any feeling, just by noticing it. Stay with it for a while. Then name it. Maybe it's a particular kind of boredom: "annoying" or "desperate" or "irksome" or "sleep-inducing." Focus on the boredom rather than letting it focus on you. Move into it. Personify it. "What do you want with me, Boredom? What are you keeping me from?"

Notice that I am making an assumption here: You are not *really* bored. Boring means uninteresting, tiresome, and dull. When you are Stopped, you are alone with yourself, and you are anything but dull. Even though you might see yourself that way, you're not. In their true self, no one is!

I believe boredom often masks fear of our virtues. Author and erstwhile presidential candidate Marianne Williamson turns fear on its ear when she wonders if just maybe what we are most deeply afraid of "is that we are powerful beyond measure. It is our light, not our darkness, that most frightens us." So perhaps your strongest fear is your wonderfulness. What a concept!

Objection: "As a child of an alcoholic mother, I never knew when it would be safe for me, so I developed an attitude of always watching out for danger. My natural inclination is to pay attention outwardly to other people, not inwardly to myself. Closing my eyes or paying attention to myself are things that make me very fearful. I'm always paying attention to everything around me to keep aware of what might be coming. I'm afraid Stopping would make me nervous."

Response: The first response, of course, is to go ahead and keep your eyes open. Closed eyes are not essential to Stopping. If it is helpful, you can substitute a trance-like stare at some point on the floor or wall or at some object, staring at it but not looking at it or seeing it. I would also suggest that you concentrate on brief Stillpoints and include with them a message of self-reassurance, a reminder that at *this* time and place you can trust the security you presume. On a deeper level, in regard to your discomfort with self-attention, I'd recommend you begin any longer expressions of Stopping by concentrating on the gifts of boundaries/openness and purpose and by examining life in your most comfortable and familiar modes: the outside and external expressions of feelings. Then, only gradually, move the focus in.

Objection: "I just can't afford the time. Yes, it's a great idea in an ideal world. Who wouldn't love to just do nothing? But the world is not ideal and there simply are more important things to do than what you describe as Stopping. No matter how beneficial, by comparison it's frivolous."

Response: Stopping can clearly challenge a person's very strongly entrenched life pattern of keeping busy, keeping going, and not looking back. What I would emphasize here are Stillpoints, literally just minutes out of the day and minutes that would normally not be useful for anything else. But I suspect it's not just the "frivolous" nature of Stopping that is objectionable, it's the very act of looking at your inner life and is fear masked as seriousness. If you feel something like this, I would suggest that you begin very gradually, just a few Stillpoints a day for a few months. Let yourself slowly get used to the act of looking in. Pick out whatever is helpful in the noticing, naming, and narrating processes, especially in the noticing.

Objection: "I'm afraid that if I stop, really Stop, like in Stopovers or Grinding Halts, I'll never be able to start again. I won't be able to get back into the fast lane, which, because of my work as an emergency room nurse, is where I spend much of my life. I am afraid that I will be permanently Stopped!"

Response: If you identify with this objection, I suggest that you treat the statement specifically as a *feeling*, not as a fact. By that I mean that the objection as stated reveals a lot of tiredness and thus its expression is, most likely, primarily an expression of a current feeling rather than a real-life fact. Probably you have done an equivalent of a Stopover sometime in your busy life and survived just fine.

By distinguishing between the feeling expressed and the actual fact, you can accept the one as a meaningful expression of what is going on with you at the moment and shine the strong light of reality on the other to test its validity. Start with Stillpoints and remember: you don't have to move on to Stopovers or Grinding Halts unless you want to. For many, Stopping will be primarily expressed in Stillpoints.

Objection: "If I do something, I do it all the way. It's like I have to do all of it or it just won't work. The same with Stopping. My inclination is to immediately do a Grinding Halt of three months. Do the most. Do the best. The rest is not worth it."

Response: This objection is the "All or Nothing" approach and is from a go-for-the-gusto kind of person who brings a lot of energy and enthusiasm to life. I would suggest that the person view Stopping not in a hierarchical, quantitative way, but in a horizontal, qualitative way. Stopping does not go from less good to best; it goes only from this way to that way with no judgment as to which way is better. So a three-month Grinding Halt is not necessarily better for this person than a few Stillpoints spread throughout the day, The way you choose to do your Stopping depends on your needs, the time available, and all the other variables of the moment. Again, start with Stillpoints.

Objection: "I want to do Stillpoints, I begin every day with the intention of doing them, but I forget. I come to the end of the day without having done even one."

Response: Here's an idea that may help. Find triggers in your day that will call you to a Stillpoint. For example, every time your phone rings, do a Stillpoint before answering it. Every time you get up from your desk (workstation, etc.), do a Stillpoint. Do this every time you go to the bathroom, get a drink of water, use the copy machine, or open a piece of mail. Can you incorporate a reminder for a Stillpoint into your screen saver? As you get in your car, before you start the ignition, or before getting out of your car, take time for a Stillpoint.

The answer to this objection has a lot to do with the idea of intentional living explored in Chapter 6. Since Stillpoints no longer just happen on their own as they used to, we must intentionally put them in our lives. Finding things that will serve as triggers will help. Above all, try not to give in to discouragement. It will take a while to incorporate Stopping into your life. Remember the benefits and stick with it.

I hope that these objections and responses will underline the central place Stillpoints hold in the process of beginning to put Stopping in your life. They are the key, the heart and the soul of learning and appreciating Stopping. Stopovers, although very effective for garnering the long-term effects of Stopping, might only come later. But Stillpoints are what will most likely get you in the habit. Gently, by accumulation, these treasured moments will bring you Stopping's gifts. They will also gradually convince you of the desirability and value of Stopovers and Grinding Halts so that you will consider using them in your life as well.

CHAPTER 39
"Stopping by Woods on a Snowy Evening"

"Normal day, let me be aware of the treasure you are. Let me learn from you, love you, bless you before you depart."

—Mary Jean Irion, author

What will Stopping look like in your life? What will help you integrate and personalize the three ways of Stopping or help you customize them by discovering your own preferences for how, when, and where Stopping is most likely to happen for you and be most beneficial?

This is the *art* of Stopping as well as where the rubber meets the road. Because if you don't actually Stop, it won't be able to work for you. The choice is yours: to continue to be overwhelmed by the problem of too much, becoming too distracted from what is really important to you—convinced, somehow, that you can't take time out even for a three-minute Stillpoint—or to begin an easy, simple, and new way of living that will bring you peace, calm, and recollection in the midst of your busy life.

Perhaps saving the best for last, here is a poem that has Stopping in the title: "Stopping by Woods on a Snowy Evening" by Robert Frost. It's a perfect poem for us at this point in the journey. For many it will be familiar. Reading it aloud will emphasize the rhythm and rhyme.

Whose woods these are I think I know.
His house is in the village though;
He will not see me stopping here
To watch his woods fill up with snow.

My little horse must think it queer
To stop without a farmhouse near
Between the woods and frozen lake
The darkest evening of the year.

He gives his harness bells a shake
To ask if there is some mistake.
The only other sound's the sweep
Of easy wind and downy flake.

The woods are lovely, dark and deep.
But I have promises to keep,
And miles to go before I sleep,
And miles to go before I sleep.

What a wonderful example of Stopping! He does nothing but stop and watch the woods fill up with snow. That is as close to doing nothing as you get. I have read the poem so often that I have a picture of the narrator in my mind. He is awake and aware of his surroundings, his aloneness in the woods, and the absence of the landowner. And he just sits quietly in the falling snow. He hears the bells, even giving them meaning as his horse's questioning. He feels the woods and names them dark, deep, and lovely.

Then he remembers: I have promises to keep and miles to go before I sleep. That's an important part of who I am, someone with promises to keep and miles to go. And then, we can assume, he returns to his life, wherever he was going when he stopped to watch, now refreshed by his Stopping. (A Christmas errand is hinted at by the "darkest evening" or winter solstice, December 21.)

All the elements of our definition are here: Stopping is doing nothing to become more fully awake and remember who you are. Sometimes I take the narrator's place and I am sitting there in my sleigh…watching the snow. Thus reading the poem becomes a Stillpoint.

We all need to discover our own unique path—the ways, times, places, triggers, occasions, and opportunities—to our "Stopping Woods," to just watch whatever is going on: falling snow or setting sun or growing grass or simply what's outside the window. What will lead you to the brief moments of Stillpoints, to the longer times of Stopovers, and to the occasional extended Stopping of a Grinding Halt?

CHAPTER 40
Permission Granted Just to Be

"If you are what you do, when you don't, you aren't."

—William Byron

Based on my Stopping seminars, I've discovered that before traveling the pathway to the Stopping Woods, it is first necessary to give everyone permission to Stop, permission to do nothing, and permission not to feel guilty.

Tinged as we are with a rigorous work ethic, a serious attitude about religion, and the general ethos of achievement, it is understandable that we still feel guilty or wrong about doing nothing. In order to incorporate Stopping into our lives, we often need permission. So if you want, and if you will give me the authority, I now grant you permission to do nothing. Here are a couple of voices to back me up:

"We all need to pause before the contemplation of our lives before we can laugh or cry. We are dying for it, literally dying for it," said the poet William Carlos Williams in 1960 shortly before he died. Notice he encourages Stopping—"pause before the contemplation of our lives"—specifically in order to be able to experience the feelings of human life, "before we can laugh or cry." When he says "we are dying for it," I believe he means it literally as well as poetically: we are ruining our health because we don't do it.

A more contemporary poet, Maya Angelou, has these words to give you permission: "Each of us needs to withdraw from the cares which will not withdraw from us. We need hours of aimless wandering or spates of time sitting on park benches, observing the mysterious world of ants and the canopy of treetops." I appreciate her image of cares that "will not withdraw from us"—as if they are stuck to us and the only way to be rid of them is with "hours of endless wanderings."

Notice that both poets use the verb *need*. This is not optional. So please take note: we—the poets and I—have now given you permission to Stop. Will you as willingly and joyfully give it to yourself? That's the real question.

In the Judeo-Christian tradition, the Sabbath is a day to rest. Whatever happened to it? Saturday and Sunday have become as rushed as any Monday. Jesus in the Christian New Testament, who frequently spent time by himself, would also spend forty days and forty nights in the desert, apart and alone. Once he even lectured Martha, who was running around doing things, saying that her sister Mary, who was doing nothing but sitting quietly, had "chosen the better part."

St. Francis was always going off by himself to contemplate, to talk to the animals, to be quiet, and to be alone. Enlightenment came to the Buddha as he was contemplating, sitting quietly under the Bodhi tree and doing nothing. The Hebrew scriptures are replete with examples of the prophets withdrawing to the desert to hear the divine voice. Indeed every religious tradition not only gives permission for what I am calling Stopping, they positively encourage it and speak of it as necessary for any life of grace.

After receiving all this permission, the act of giving *yourself* permission to Stop can lead you to the important developmental discovery of the difference between being a *human doing* and being a *human being*. Giving yourself permission is an act of authority by you and over you. It emphasizes that you are a *you* and not an *it* or an *act*.

William Byron's quote at the start of this chapter points out the danger we all run of being a human doing: if you so identify with what you do—teaching, nursing, repairing, doctoring, cleaning, driving, lawyering, doing business, or whatever you do—then when you are not doing that particular work, you no longer have a sense of who you are; quite literally, you stop being and you lose yourself. On the other hand, if you keep your work as something, albeit a very important something, that you *do*, then you are free to continue *to be* who you have always been and will continue to be no matter what happens in your life.

Medical professors David Waters and Terry Saunders tell of this incident: In frustration a woman asked her husband, a busy physician, "What is it you get at work that you don't get at home?" He thought for a minute and answered, "It's the only time I really feel like I know who I am." Here is a man for whom being and doing are the same thing. This common problem often becomes evident at the moment of changing jobs or at retirement, or simply when going home every evening.

I can identify with the feelings of the physician as I recall my process of leaving the ministry. Was it something I was or something I did? I am still in the process of getting the full answer to that question.

So please give yourself permission, maybe quite frequently, to do nothing and to Stop. It is a permission that will lead you to *be* who you are and want to become, and then to *do* whatever you do.

CHAPTER 41
The Pathway to Your Stopping Woods

"My soul can find no staircase to heaven unless it be through earth's loveliness."

—Michelangelo, artist

To find more answers on how to make Stopping a natural part of your life, come with me through "earth's loveliness" and along the path to the place that will make Stopping easy and enjoyable for you and where you are most likely to actually do it: your Stopping Woods. Along the way, we'll come across some suggestions to help you not only arrive at your Stopping Woods safely but be able to visit there whenever you want.

The idea is to pick whatever things will help you create your own Stopping. I suggest you put a mark by the things that attract your attention or sound enjoyable to you: those that you know have helped you in the past and those you want to cultivate. These things will help you get to your Stopping Woods. Make your selections thoughtfully, and by the end of this short journey you will probably find that you have the main components—and thus a description—of your personal practice of Stopping.

Reading

What do you read that encourages Stopping or that enhances your meanings and values? All major spiritual traditions have their scriptures or sacred writings: The Torah, the New Testament, the Quran, the Upanishads, the Bhagavad Gita, and others. Would you pick one of these or part of one, such as the Psalms of the Old Testament, the Four Noble Truths of Buddhism, or the Gospel of Mark? Prayer books, containing familiar prayers, psalms, and other sacred texts might be something also to consider. Repetitive reading of favorite texts brings a sense of continuity and familiarity that is important to many.

Small books of daily thoughts or brief aphorisms have become popular in recent years. These are the perfect companions of Stopping. Each day brings a new, provocative, and brief statement that you can use in your Stillpoints throughout the day. You might open a book at random and read what is there as your thought for the day; and each time you do a Stillpoint, you recall your thought.

The Latin term *lectio divina*—literally "divine reading" but most often translated as "spiritual reading"—can refer to any reading that deepens your spiritual life, your connection with the divine, or your life of meanings and values. For some, these will be works written specifically for a religious or spiritual purpose, for others, it may also consist of novels or short stories. It may be anything.

As you might guess, poetry is often *lectio divina* for me. Reading a brief poem and letting it have its way with me will often be what doing nothing looks like for me during an afternoon Stopover.

What is spiritual reading for you? Don't limit yourself to only the expected sources. Anything goes.

Writing

Does anyone write letters anymore? A regular correspondence with a friend can be a wonderful help for Stopping because you have to pause regularly in the process to stop and think about what you want to say and how.

Email, texting, IMs, tweets, Snapchat, Instagram, and all of the social media sites are becoming the contemporary equivalent of letters through the mail. After all, our Stopping is at the speed of light and these means are fast. But remember: just because they are fast, they don't have to be unthoughtful or hurried.

Instead of reading a poem, you can spend a Stopover writing a poem. Why not keep a book of your own poetry?

My brother wrote a forty-page booklet consisting of twenty stories from his life and gave copies to his family for whom they are a treasure and will be for generations to come. Those stories will tell them something about themselves. I have a niece who has a packet of finished and not-quite-finished short stories tucked away in her desk. For many writers of personal stories, the writing is more important than anyone reading them. It reminds us, and we remember.

Journals and diaries are the classic forms of personal writing and are wonderful ways to record the meanings and values of your life. They are the perfect companions, especially for the longer times of Stopping. To write down the events and feelings of life is to notice them, to give them importance, and to keep them.

Maybe you will just want to collect your own favorite words, phrases, or epigraphs (like the ones at the beginning of the chapters in this book), and keep them in a special place, in a journal, or on your computer.

Visual Beauty

"Without beauty there's little fun and less humor," said James Hillman. To that I will add, "Without beauty there's impoverished spirituality." For mature human life, beauty, in all its forms, is not optional, and I believe neglect of beauty is one of our most serious and hidden faults. President Kennedy was aware of this when he said one month before he died, "I look forward to an America which will not be afraid of grace and beauty." Beauty needs no intermediary to get to the human soul. It scores a direct hit and stimulates what is best, most noble, and most enjoyable in us. Those artistic souls who bring us beauty are our greatest treasures. Too often we benignly ignore them, commercialize them, or, sometimes, stone them.

"Somewhere, amid the darkness, a painter measures a blank canvas, a poet tests a line aloud, a songwriter brings a melody into tune. Art inspires, provokes thought, reflects beauty and pain. I seek it out even more in these times. And in so doing, I find hope in the human spirit."
—Dan Rather, newscaster

How can you gather beauty? Don't be limited to just the suggestions here. Are there beautiful pictures in your daily life? Cost is no excuse with all the inexpensive reproductions available. It certainly does not have to be by a famous artist and is better if it's by you. How often do you go to the art museum, a beautiful church, or an architectural gem of a building in your town or city? These (or their equivalents) are not optional niceties, but essential parts of our day for a balanced life, and they are gateways to Stopping. What is beautiful to you? Beauty is in the eye of the beholder. Add it—or a representation of it—to your life.

What colors do you love? Are they all around you? What better way to lift your spirits than to paint your room a new color?

Pin up a photograph or a painting by your computer and let this visual cue lead you to moments—or hours—of Stopping.

Touching

There are so many times we can touch each other. Handshakes, hugs, pats on the back, or a gentle hand on the arm; all of these can be a moment of pausing, and, with attention, each can become a Stillpoint. Here's a suggestion: make every hug a Stillpoint. Breathe, notice where you are, and notice what is important to you. (Of course, under the influence of the "Me Too" movement and any health pandemic, considerations of appropriateness and safety must be observed.)

The textures of cloth on your hand, of food in your mouth, or of anything sensory can signal complexity, simplicity, involvement, or detachment. As you pick up a roughly woven sweater or a smooth silk scarf, your Stillpoint message might be: "Just like the feel of this weave, there are rough spots in my life right now, but I'll be okay, I'll take care of myself"; or "May my challenging day turn out to be as smooth as this silk."

Eating meals can be a moment of quiet recognition of our dependence on food and our gratitude for having it. The beginning of a meal is an especially good time to pause for grace. When you eat with others, family or friends, could you call everyone to a moment of pause or reflection—a shared Stillpoint? Martin Buber reminds us that when "one eats in holiness…the table becomes an altar."

Fast food is what we often eat. Constantly eating fast food is not only contrary to being awake and remembering, it can actually induce spiritual sleep. In Europe, there is an organization called Slow Food: The International Movement for the Defense of and the Right to Pleasure. It was started after McDonalds set up shop in Paris. But fast food is not going away, because it is so cheap and convenient and fits with the other elements of our lives. So when you find yourself grabbing that burger, chugging that soda, or inhaling that pizza, let it serve as a reminder: a fast food Stillpoint. Your stomach will thank you and the people you meet the rest of the day will thank you.

And let's remember: eating a meal relatively quickly is not necessarily bad. I believe it is possible to eat a healthy lunch in a healthy way in a short time if it's done with attention and relaxation. Incessantly eating too fast, not being able to control the speed, timing, and amount of leisure around a meal, and inhaling food with no thoughtfulness of the process—those are bad.

Sexuality can be expressed not only in the moments of lovemaking but in all of the moments of life. You experience it daily as gendered person, with your particular sensuality and your way of seeing, touching, and appreciating. Erotic energy has accomplished, and will continue to accomplish, wonders for humanity and can lead you to delightful and delicious moments of sexually charged reveries: passionate Stillpoints. From my experience—as a therapist as well as a sexual being—spirituality and sexuality are neighboring facets on the same gem. In the presence of the power of one, the power of the other is always close at hand.

Beautiful Sounds and Fragrances

I agree with Nietzsche, who said that "life would be a mistake without music," and with Aldous Huxley, who said, "After silence, that which comes nearest to expressing the inexpressible is music." I can't imagine life without it. What about you?

"Music is the mediator between spiritual and the sensual life."
—Ludwig van Beethoven, composer

My friend Michael is uncontrollably transported by the sound of certain music. We've been in the middle of a conversation when his eyes roll up in his head, his head tilts back, his arms rise, he begins mouthing the lyrics, and he is somewhere else. An aria from *Madama Butterfly* is playing in the background and Michael is "gone" for a moment. This is an example of the direct hit that beauty makes on the soul and why it is so necessary. It doesn't have to be filtered through the intellect. It is pure, experienced joy.

When you have a moment, search for the "second movement of Beethoven's Fifth Piano Concerto" on your computer and simply spend a few moments listening. Vivaldi's *Gloria* is a piece that always scores a direct hit on me. When the combined choruses build to a crescendo of glorious sounds, I'm transported to a pure moment of pleasure: a transcendent Stillpoint.

The sound of a particular voice: Does that lead you to a moment of Stopping? How about the sounds of the ocean, of foghorns, of the wind, of birds, of whales, of trains, or of ships? One of my favorite sounds in the world, and one that will freeze-frame me into a most enjoyable Stillpoint, is the distant sound of a loon on a northern lake.

Aromatherapy is popular these days but certainly nothing new. Humans and animals have always used scent to attract each other. What are your favorite fragrances? Will burning incense, potpourri, or scented candles lead you to Stopping?

Scents can be powerful reminders of the past, evoking emotions and memories that can lead us to quiet moments of reverie.

Sacramentals

One of the qualities I appreciate about the Catholic tradition is its principle of sacramentality. That is, as theologian Richard McBrien defines it, "the notion that all reality, both animate and inanimate, is potentially or in fact the bearer of divine presence." Thus food, oil, trees, the sun, the moon, the stars, cocker spaniels, new cars, rosebuds, talismans, charms, and shiny stones—things we can taste, touch, or smell—can bring us into contact with the cosmic and universal. Soulful objects in the valley connect us with transcendent moments on the peaks. Many other religious traditions also embody this principle.

Sacramentals are also personal objects that symbolize something that has great spiritual value or meaning to us. Your grandfather's watch or your mother's ring, perhaps. Anything, really, that symbolizes a value. Think of the things you own and which of them is a sacramental for you. Every time you see it or hold it: a Stillpoint.

Rituals

Rituals bestow a sheltered time and space in which to pause and reflect on life's changing moments as well as offering chances to make sense out of both the familiar and the mysterious. There are the common family rituals of birthday cakes, wedding celebrations, bedtime stories, and good-night kisses, and religious rituals like baptism, bar mitzvah, the mass, the seder, and the many forms of prayer such as novenas, devotions, and making the sign of the cross. If you take just a moment, I'm sure you can think of rituals that are unique to your family. All of these can be a lead into a Stopping experience because they bring you to a moment or moments of quiet and they are reminders of who you are that can awaken you to the present.

But what about bringing ritual to the more common moments of life? What about creating your personal rituals around the events that carry meaning for you? Do you have rituals around exercise or eating or sleeping or vacations or Sunday mornings or, perhaps, the day you made a life-changing decision? Note the occasion with a simple remembering ritual, perhaps a recollection, a prayer, a brief visit to a place, or the lighting of a candle. At dinner, remind your family or meal companion(s) what anniversary this is—the day Grandfather died, the day your child was baptized, or a day important to the ethnicity of your family—and invite them to a moment of quiet reflection on the event so that everyone enjoys a Stillpoint together.

At those times when you are eating alone, it is especially rewarding to recall some meaningful event or person and ritualize it by unobtrusively toasting with your cup of tea or inviting them to join you in spirit for this meal.

Spaces and Places

At a particular point on the trail I often follow in the park near my home, there is one place where I can see Mount Tamalpais to the west across the Bay and Mount Diablo to the east. It is a sacred place for me. I pause every time I pass the spot, and I take time for a Stillpoint.

Mountains? Deserts? Which calls to you? Where are you most at home and most yourself? To which of the natural places do you head when you want comfort, consolation, and acceptance?

I feel fortunate to live on the Northern California coast, a blessed place if ever there was one. The Pacific Ocean is astounding, no matter the time of day or year; it calls to the deep in us. Lakes, rivers, and for many, like Thoreau, even ponds can be sacred places of quiet and meaning. "I went to [Walden Pond] because I wished to live deliberately…" Do you have a Walden Pond? A Walden River? A Walden Lake?

For many people, sacred spaces are of human origin: museums or churches, for example. For me the rotunda at the National Gallery of Art in Washington, DC, is such a place. When I'm there I feel transported to another level and experience a feeling of calm and appreciation. Why? I don't know. Who is not struck dumb on entering the cathedral in Florence? Or even, perhaps, a small church in your neighborhood?

Animals

What joy animals can bring to our lives! One only has to watch a boy with his dog, a grandmother with her cat, or perhaps you with your pet to know the power of animal connection. We know that holding an animal can bring calm and a sense of well-being. If you have a pet, touching or petting or otherwise connecting with it can be the most consistent and rewarding way of integrating Stillpoints into your daily life. Make it your intention that every time you connect with your pet, you will take a breath, be aware of the moment, and bring to mind what you need to remember.

You can see an animal as a totem, as an emblem of your own self, or as a guardian spirit. For years my niece and I have been wilderness traveling companions, needing no excuse to get a group together and strike out in canoes or kayaks. During those excursions we have come to know our totems as the bear (mine) and the dolphin (hers). They have become meaningful symbols, emblems of what we need or appreciate in our lives and of what we want to achieve.

Seasons, Weather, and Movements of the Earth

Winter, spring, summer, fall, rain, sun, wind, fog, snow, hail, mist, holy days, liturgical seasons, holiday seasons, or family birthdays: all of these and many more can be occasions for Stillpoints and sometimes for Stopovers as well. All these seasons and conditions are pregnant with meaning—the coziness of winter, new life of spring, playfulness of summer, and the advancing darkness of autumn.

Every day of every year offers many occasions for Stillpoints merely by noticing that we are outside or by noticing the calendar or season and letting them lead you to what you need in the moment.

I still recall a moment from years ago: It was a beautifully clear and crisp night in spring. We were seated in a restaurant's outdoor portico with a fire crackling in the fireplace nearby. To the east, I looked up to watch an eclipse of the moon; to the west, I looked up to watch a comet soaring through space. The combination of visible cosmic drama, a significant birthday, perfect company, and the beauty of the place provided me not only with several Stillpoints that evening, but with many more, even to this moment, in the remembering.

This listing—this journey down the pathway to your Stopping Woods—is just a hint of what can call you to a time of Stopping. Be sure to spend a moment gathering your thoughts or making a list of the kinds of things that especially call you. They might not be the expected things like holy objects or seasons of the year; they may even seem quite odd.

One of mine is fishponds. When I was very young—maybe four or five, Petey, a little boy down the street who was younger than I, drowned in the fishpond in his backyard. It was my first encounter with death, and it happened in a place with which I was familiar and where I had often played. It had a profound effect on me. From that day to this, I don't see or hear of a fishpond without thinking briefly of Petey and the fragility of life and the need to make every moment count: a Stillpoint.

Does anything come to your mind that might be an unusual trigger for your Stopping? Perhaps you can keep your list handy and continue your process of defining how you will incorporate Stopping into your daily routine.

CHAPTER 42

Stopping While Moving

"You can't get there from here."

—Ogden Nash, poet

Especially when you are thinking that poet Ogden Nash's words make perfect sense and Stopping feels like something that you can't get to from where you are now, it is important to remember this: Stopping often takes place most easily during a time of transition, of movement from one event to another or from one place to another. Whether it is a Stillpoint between appointments, on the way to or from work, on a Stopover weekend between work weeks, or on a Grinding Halt between life stages, it is a powerful "pause between the notes." To identify your most common transitions is a significant step toward incorporating Stopping into your life.

I suppose the most typical transition time for many people is the daily commute. For commuters, Stillpoints can transform this time from horror to haven. If you were to see these moments (or for some, hours) of transition as welcome pauses or rests wherein you can Stop, you might even look forward to them.

If you drive your car to work, you are probably thinking, as I have often thought, "In that horrible traffic, as tired and hot as I often feel, as frustrating as my day has been, how could I possibly look forward to that time?" But it is possible to incorporate Stillpoints into your drive. And believe me: you'll feel better.

Obviously, the only parts of the Stillpoint that won't work while driving are the optional parts of closing your eyes and diverting your attention or anything which would endanger you on the road. Your first concern must be to remain alert and attentive to the act of driving. But there is still much you can do within those parameters. The driving Stillpoint will be less introspective and will be more geared to your physical and mental comfort.

"Being still does not mean don't move. It means move in peace."
—E'yen Gardner, poet

Recall the idea from part I about intentional living: the need to take the things of daily life out of the realm of habitual routine and into the realm of conscious choice. It applies here: You can intentionally turn drive time into Stopping time. Choose to consciously breathe every time you reach a red light or stop sign or every time a driver is rude or dangerous. Choose music that soothes, choose the Stillpoint message you need to hear, choose to use positive vocabulary when talking and thinking of commuting, and, lastly, choose to see your commute time not as horrible and something you have to endure, but as valuable and something that enhances your life, your powerful pause, and your rest between the notes. From now on, drive time is Stillpoint time.

Trains, buses, airplanes, and boats all are ideal places for Stillpoints. They have the advantage of leaving the driving to someone else so that your Stillpoints can be more complete and effective.

What are some other transition times in your life? Every day is filled with them: from sleep to waking, from bathroom to bedroom, from breakfast to the car, from school to work, and from weekday to weekend. In other words, transition time is *from* any one thing or place or time *to* any other thing or place or time; they are all the "from-to's" of your life.

So whenever it feels like you can't get from here (wherever you are) to there (Stopping), think of transitions. What are you in between? Where are you coming from? Where are you going? What was last and what is next? As the nature and needs of your transitions are identified, the specific way of Stopping will also become clear.

Moving Your Body

There are some people who just have a very difficult time keeping still, that is, maintaining their body in a nonmoving mode for any length of time. This immediately makes me think of Carla. When I am with her, I am constantly aware that she never stops jiggling her legs, moving here, going there, or gesticulating unendingly. She has a very hard time staying still. There's nothing at all wrong with that; it's her metabolism. Whenever I feel anxious, I can identify with Carla: I don't want to sit still, it bothers me, and I need to move.

Thoreau understands Carla, too. In his essay "Walking," he says, "I think that I cannot preserve my health and spirits, unless I spend four hours a day at least—and it is commonly more than that—sauntering through the woods and over the fields." For all of us, Stopping can be done while moving.

How about jogging-Stopping? This would seem more challenging, at least for me, but maybe not for you. I think it would be difficult to maintain a quality of calm and attentiveness while moving quickly. Thoreau slows walking down to sauntering; running or jogging speeds it up. Recalling the equation of "Speed is to forgetting as slowness is to remembering" would seem to bear this out.

Working out in a gym or at home would seem to fall into the same speed category. There is a lot of physical exertion and concentration involved. I think these high-energy activities could start with, pause in the middle for, and end with Stillpoints, and thus transform the entire exercise experience into something beyond physical development. But this surely is a matter of individual preference.

During a recent workshop, I asked how people had experienced Stopping in their lives. Immediately Bill spoke up and said, "On the golf course." He explained his inward state of mind, his peacefulness, and how, by focusing on hitting the ball, he is free to let everything else go. "I often have to be reminded that it's my turn to play."

There is another important way to move and Stop at the same time: pacing. I discovered pacing when I was a student, and I have used it regularly since then. Pacing is slowly walking a predetermined and repetitive course while mentally concentrating on something else. The Buddhists call this walking meditation.

You might like to try pacing. I find it especially helpful when I am feeling anxious or nervous for any reason. Pick out a safe course, inside or outside. The course must be predictable, safe, and repeatable. Pace back and forth in your room or office, in a circle in the yard, in a park, or anywhere; you don't need a lot of room for this. Rather than close your eyes, you can cast them down at the ground. The moving seems to soothe the anxiety and because your course is safe and predictable—you don't have to pay attention to where you are physically going—you can in fact be still in your soul: a Stillpoint.

The ultimate in pacing is the labyrinth. The labyrinth is an ancient, universal image of life on the floor/ground, a large circle with a clear, winding path from the outside to the center and back. (Not to be confused with a maze, which has blind ends and tricks.) A local medical center, which has a labyrinth in its courtyard for its patients and staff, calls it "a sacred path to health and wholeness." People are encouraged to walk, run, or dance—most walk slowly—in and out of the sacred circle.

Dr. Lauren Artress of San Francisco's Grace Cathedral is mainly responsible for bringing the ancient practice to contemporary awareness. In her book *Walking a Sacred Path: Rediscovering the Labyrinth as a Spiritual Tool,* she describes the labyrinth as offering "a sacred and stable place to focus the attention and listen to the longing of the soul" and as a "tool to guide healing, deepen self-knowledge and empower creativity."

Walking the labyrinth is the epitome of moving while Stopping. Dr. Artress says that for many who have walked the labyrinth—and I am one of them—"time seems to stand still." Yes! There! That's it! (See labyrinthlocator.com to find a local labyrinth.)

CHAPTER 43

The Young, the Old, and the Angry

"To live is so startling it leaves little time for anything else."

—Emily Dickinson, poet

At this point I hope you get the idea that Stopping is a very adaptable process. People tend to develop their own style, and any given person might well practice Stopping in different ways at different times. There are very few rules and no dogmas at all; that is, Stopping has no content in the form of beliefs or doctrines. It is pure process and can fit with any spiritual system or with none and with any person's style. The idea is simply to achieve enough quiet and enough stillness to hear the truth, both within and without.

Some folks will prefer to keep moving during their Stillpoints, while others will prefer to stay physically still. Some will be on a golf course and some will be in a chapel.

For Stopovers, some will stay home, and others will go far away. Some will be attracted to the long times of Grinding Halts and do them several times in their lives, while others will never do one. Some will…well, you get the idea. Please keep in mind however, that the great thing about Stillpoints is that *you can do them in any way, in any place, and at any time.*

There are three groups of people for whom Stopping offers special implications and challenges. They are the young, the old, and the angry/violent.

Children and Adolescents

The general assumption of this book is that we are speaking to and about adults. But both adolescents and children need Stopping as much as we do and, in some ways, they can teach us a lot about it.

If you have any experience with adolescents, you know that they can be very spacey or distracted from what you think they should be attending to. Although frustrating, it's a normal and important part of their development, and, in a manner of speaking, it is one of their ways of Stopping, of taking time out from all the challenges of their rapidly changing lives, and of trying to remember who they are and what's important to them. Because we associate it with the awkward and frustrating years of adolescence, we miss the value of doing our own variety of spacing out; it might feel too juvenile.

And, of course, the Stopping ability of young children is legendary. One need only watch a lone child at play to notice and learn.

We need to take lessons from the younger members of our families. Really though, it is not a lesson we need to learn as much as it is a memory and a practice we need to recapture, for we too were their age and had their same native expertise. Only we lost it.

More than anything, we adults can help by creating times, places, and opportunities for Stopping for the young people in our lives. Help them notice the pauses between their notes and the value of them. Of course the first comment your efforts might bring is, "Mom, I'm bored!" or "Dad, there's nothing to do!" but with persistence, and especially with example on our part, they can learn the value of Stopping.

The Elderly

The real pros at Stopping are old people. In the dedication of this book, I indicate that my father was an example to me of how to use Stopping. This was most especially true in his later years. He enjoyed over twenty years of retirement and was very content doing very little and spending many hours simply Stopped. As he went through his losses—athletic ability, sufficient eyesight for reading, and adequate hearing for normal conversation—he just remained quiet, contemplating and remembering.

My father was not one to tell you his feelings at any great length, but when he did, it was often worth noting. My mother tells this story: One evening, just a few years before Dad's death at ninety-one, my parents were sitting in their chairs, as they did every evening. Probably my mother was reading, and Dad was just sitting quietly. Out of the blue he said to her, "You know, dear, I think I need a computer." My mother literally dropped her book in amazement and exclaimed, "A computer? What on earth for?" My father's response: "To count my blessings."

The challenge is to get smart before we get too old—too old to learn or even to change. By developing Stopping now, our years of old age and loss are much more likely to be sweet and calm; you won't be a dear old man or woman unless you are continually becoming a dear younger one. Old Scrooge, in Dickens's *A Christmas Carol,* really had it easy. Only three terrifying visitors in one miserable night and he became a new man. For the rest of us, it's night by night and day by day.

The Angry and Violent

I have no idea what to do about the incredible violence that we visit upon ourselves. I watch in amazement and horror the TV news and even ads for movies and television programs filled with terrible human anger and violence, and I read the many news items of murder and mayhem. I know that I am not the only one who feels this way; most of the people I speak with feel the same. It must be because people in power believe that money is always the bottom line and this stuff sells. But why does it sell? I still have no real answer...except Stopping. It is at least a start.

At first that seems a very naive answer. But when I think it through, I come to a point of conviction: The only thing that will change the pattern and habit of violence in people is the only thing that has ever morally transformed people— conversion; a turning around of the way one sees things. To do that, we must help people Stop, because Stopping is a necessary condition for a change of heart. You can't change if you are not still enough, long enough, to see that there is a different way or a better way. Angry and violent people—that's all of us, potentially—are so hugely and profoundly distracted that a better way is literally unimaginable.

Let the youth on the street Stop. Let the war mongers Stop. Let the network CEOs Stop. Let politicians and world leaders Stop. Let the newspaper editors Stop. Let parents Stop. Let the teachers Stop. Let the men Stop. Let the women Stop. Let the children Stop. Let me and you Stop.

CHAPTER 44
Caring and Trusting

"Caring is the greatest thing, caring matters most."
—Friedrich Von Hügel, author

I believe at this point it is evident that Stopping aims to access those most personal issues, feelings, and truths that are in the heart and soul of each of us and that help us to realize our purpose, and to help us know who we are and what and who is important to us. But Stopping, especially if you stick with it for a while, goes beyond those questions to the bigger, broader ones that affect the world. In fact, in looking at our most personal issues and desires, we can thereby naturally be led out of ourselves to the needs of the world's communities. Stopping always leads to caring.

Stopping can bolster your trust in yourself so that when you are confronted with the question, "Is the story I'm telling crazy, or is the rest of the world crazy?" you will be able to answer truthfully, "It's the rest of the world!" Carl Jung acknowledged it years ago. Craziness today has been institutionalized. Our citizens, individually, are for the most part sane and reasonable; it's our institutions that are nuts! And we take on that craziness because we have to work within the framework of these institutions.

The popularity of the comic strip *Dilbert* is a perfect example of our recognition of this, it points out the absurdity of his company's rules and procedures as well as their continued existence. Let's hope corporate craziness is a phase and is, perhaps, a necessary step in reaching for flexible systems that put people first. Developing the habit of Stopping will help continue to convince you of your sanity.

A Final Encouragement:

To facilitate and speed up your practice of Stopping, do your best to emphasize *Stopovers*, those little-bit-longer times of Stopping: a whole afternoon, a day, a weekend. Why not plan a Stopover right now, as you finish reading this book? Get out your calendar and make a note.

This idea has a corollary for people with the responsibility of children. With all the talk of dysfunctional families going on these days, I hope that Stopping leads us to recognize that all systems to one degree or another are dysfunctional. *And that many families are quite functional* and send their children out into very dysfunctional—that is crazy—social systems and worldly institutions. A family, no matter how it is configured, that Stops, is a family more prepared to face that contemporary reality and still thrive.

Lastly, I hope that it is clear by now: Stopping is fundamentally optimistic and hopeful. The process of Stopping is based on the belief that you are perfectly fine just the way you are and that you will continue to discover more and more of your own truth, beauty, and goodness as you incorporate the practice of Stopping into your life.

Acknowledgments

I want to express my sincere thanks and appreciation to:

Mary Elyn Bahlert and Jeff Kunkel who read and helped with the original text; to Chilton Thomson (RIP), an extraordinary teacher, who many years ago was the first to call forth from my soul a desire for reading and writing; to Robert Stenberg, in whom I recognized and appreciated the use and value of Stillpoints; and to Mary Jane Ryan, Jan Johnson, Brenda Knight, Natasha Vera, and to all the great folks at Conari Press—thanks.

Permissions

The author gratefully acknowledges the authors and publishers who gave permission to reprint the following works:

The poem, "What If" by Ganga White in Chapter 8 is used by permission: (c) 2007 Ganga White, All Rights Reserved, Used with permission. whitelotus.org.

"Stopping by Woods on a Snowy Evening," from *The Poetry of Robert Frost,* edited by Edward Connery Lathem. Copyright 1951 by Robert Frost, copyright 1923, © 1969 by Henry Holt & Co., Inc. Reprinted by permission of Henry Holt & Co., Inc.

Quotes from C.G. Jung in Chapter 39 from *Memories, Dreams, Reflections* by C. G. Jung, translated by Richard & Clara Winston. Translation copyright © 1961, 1962, 1963 and renewed 1989, 1990, 1991 by Random House, Inc. Reprinted by permission of Pantheon Books, a division of Random House, Inc.

Excerpts from *Slowness* by Milan Kundera © 1995 by Milan Kundera. Translation copyright © 1996 by Linda Asher. Published by HarperCollins, Inc.

"Beyond living and dreaming…" reprinted from *Times Alone: Selected Poems of Antonio Machado,* trans. by Robert Bly, Wesleyan University Press, Middletown, CT 1983. Copyright © 1983 by Robert Bly. Reprinted with his permission.

About the Author

David J. Kundtz is an author, speaker, and marriage and family therapist (retd.). He began his psychotherapy career at a social service agency in Oakland, CA, before conducting a private counseling practice in Berkeley, CA, for some twenty years. He was director of Inside Track Seminars, offering workshops in the areas of human resources, stress management, and emotional health. Prior to that he was in ordained ministry in the Catholic Diocese of Boise, Idaho, also serving in Cali, Colombia, South America.

He has earned graduate degrees in psychology and theology and his doctoral degree, a Doctor of Science and theology (SThD), is in the field of pastoral psychology. He is a member of the California Association of Marriage and Family Therapists. His other books include *Quiet Mind: One Minute Mindfulness*, *Nothing's Wrong: A Man's Guide to Managing His Feelings*,

Awakened Mind: One Minute Wake Up Calls, Being Present: A Book of Daily Reflections, and *Coming To: A Biomythograhpy.* He lives in Kensington, California.

Dr. Kundtz warmly welcomes your communication, especially your experiences, insights, challenges, and successes with Stopping.

Send email to: dk@stopping.com

Visit the Stopping web site at: www.stopping.com

Mango Publishing, established in 2014, publishes an eclectic list of books by diverse authors—both new and established voices—on topics ranging from business, personal growth, women's empowerment, LGBTQ studies, health, and spirituality to history, popular culture, time management, decluttering, lifestyle, mental wellness, aging, and sustainable living. We were recently named 2019 *and* 2020's #1 fastest-growing independent publisher by *Publishers Weekly*. Our success is driven by our main goal, which is to publish high-quality books that will entertain readers as well as make a positive difference in their lives.

Our readers are our most important resource; we value your input, suggestions, and ideas. We'd love to hear from you—after all, we are publishing books for you!

Please stay in touch with us and follow us at:

Facebook: Mango Publishing

Twitter: @MangoPublishing

Instagram: @MangoPublishing

LinkedIn: Mango Publishing

Pinterest: Mango Publishing

Newsletter: mangopublishinggroup.com/newsletter

Join us on Mango's journey to reinvent publishing, one book at a time.